Opera
Guide

Il Trovatore

Verdi

Pauline Viardot as Azucena at Covent Garden in 1855. 'She is a true Gipsy, exhibiting the peculiar features and passions of her race. Nothing can be more artistic than her singing, though the extraordinary power of her acting throws it in the shade' — but the 'story is revolting, horrible, confused, and full of gross improbabilities'. (Theatre Museum)

Preface

This series, published under the auspices of English National Opera and The Royal Opera, aims to prepare audiences to enjoy and evaluate opera performances. Each book contains the complete text, set out in the original language together with a current performing translation. The accompanying essays have been commissioned as general introductions to aspects of interest in each work. As many illustrations and musical examples as possible have been included because the sound and spectacle of opera are clearly central to any sympathetic appreciation of it. We hope that, as companions to the opera should be, they are well-informed, witty and attractive.

ENO is very grateful to British Olivetti Limited for sponsoring this Guide to *Il Trovatore*, as part of its wide-ranging programme of support for the arts.

Nicholas John
Series Editor

Il Trovatore

Giuseppe Verdi

Opera Guide Series Editor: Nicholas John

Published in association with
English National Opera and The Royal Opera
This Guide is sponsored by British Olivetti Limited

John Calder · London
Riverrun Press · New York

Contents

List of Illustrations

First published in Great Britain, 1983, by
John Calder (Publishers) Ltd, 18 Brewer Street,
London W1R 4AS

and

First published in the U.S.A., 1983, by
Riverrun Press Inc.,
175 Fifth Avenue
New York, NY 10010

BRITISH LIBRARY CATALOGUING IN PUBLICATION DATA
Verdi, Giuseppe
  Il trovatore.—(Opera guides; 20)
  1. Verdi, Giuseppe. Trovatore, Il   2. Operas—Librettos
  I. Title   II. Cammarano, Salvatore
  III. John, Nicholas   IV. Series
  782.1'2   ML50,V484

  ISBN 0-7145-3877-9

SUBSIDISED BY THE
Arts Council
OF GREAT BRITAIN

John Calder (Publishers) Ltd, English National Opera and
The Royal Opera House, Covent Garden Ltd. receive financial
assistance from the Arts Council of Great Britain. English
National Opera also receives financial assistance from the
Greater London Council.

Typeset in Plantin by Margaret Spooner Typesetting, Dorchester, Dorset.

Printed in Great Britain by Whitstable Litho Ltd., Whitstable, Kent.

'Higher than the highest, the music better than the best'

Pascarella, a Roman dialect poet

Marcello Conati
translated by Jonathan Keates

What exactly is *Il Trovatore?*

'The definitive melodramma', asserted Bruno Barilli: 'its scenes make up the ultimate challenge (*'la Via Crucis'*) of Italian song'.[1] While Massimo Mila has only recently called it 'the most absurd and far-fetched of all'[2], Alberto Savinio considers it 'Verdi's masterpiece. In none of his other works is the inspiration so lofty. None of the others can boast arias of such remoteness, of such soaring purity ... lonely kites soaring through the strange calm of a windless sky into an endless night.'[3]

As for Cammarano's libretto, all too often labelled tasteless, abstruse, incomprehensible ...? For Savinio it becomes 'the highest, the most inspired Verdi ever placed upon his piano. Less an opera libretto than an oratorio text, offering the composer a succession of sound pictures ... Some of Cammarano's lines in *Trovatore* achieve the highest peaks of poetry.' For Gabriele Baldini it is 'the ideal libretto for music', of the sort which guarantees 'to the full a musical existence for each character with nothing beyond it, in effect a phantom libretto' to be 'swallowed by the music ... Thus, in fact, the *Trovatore* libretto has disappeared and no-one has ever been able to trace it.'[4]

And what of Verdi's supposed 'vulgarity', that 'depraved aesthetic instinct', that 'fraudulent, deliberate quest for the commonplace' with which the 19th-century Austrian critic Hanslick reproached him? To this the most illuminating response is Alberto Moravia's — although it is less of a response than a working hypothesis: 'We believe that vulgarity (*'volgarità'*) is perhaps the most mysterious and perplexing aspect of Verdi's character ... This is the humanist concept central to our Renaissance, forsaken and betrayed by the Italian governing classes after the Counter-Reformation, but preserved among the common people and reduced to folklore.'[5]

What, then, does *Il Trovatore* represent? Students, critics and writers are carried away with enthusiasm whenever they discuss this archetype of Verdian theatre. Few have described so vividly as Bruno Barilli the impressions evoked by its 'scarlet music' and 'gothic surrealism':

> What does *Il Trovatore* represent? It seeks simply to exist as itself — to be left alone — for us not to approach it with a guide in our pocket or a notebook and pen in our hand ... *Il Trovatore* is like a being that desires to be born without mother, midwife or obstetrician [. . . .] to be its own autonomous self like a baby with a number but no address or relations ... a swaddled and defenceless bundle, perhaps, left on the

[1] *Il paese del melodramma e altri scritti musicale* ed. Enrico Falqui, 1963, Vellechi, Florence
[2] *La giovinezza di Verdi*, Torino 1978, Einaudi
[3] *Scatola sonora*, Milan 1955, Ricordi
[4] See bibliography
[5] *L'uomo come fine e eltri saggi*, Milan 1964, Bompiani

Adelina Patti as Leonora at Covent Garden in 1863 (Theatre Museum): 'her acting with Signor Mario in the last two scenes was worthy of Rachel'.

threshold of time. Obviously, when faced with this opera that defies comparison, critics become totally and irredeemably confused. This is where Verdi's art, which is all in subversion, deformation, sublime caricature, sets the four corners of the world on fire. Anyone used to sticking his fingers into the inner workings of a piece of music just because he thinks he knows it well, is likely to pull them out here and jump back with a shock from the fierce explosive charge within.

Famous words, often re-read, full of ideas even for those of us who mistrust literary images and would rather follow Savinio's advice that *Trovatore* 'must be treated with care, delicacy and prudence, like a newly-excavated statue'.

Meddling with its workings is far more delicate and difficult than with *Otello* or *Tristan*. As Pierluigi Petrobelli says:

> We must search for an explanation of the opera's cohesive strength (. . . .) in its basic construction, and in the relationships established by the composer within the score.*

By careful scrutiny of such elements *Trovatore* will emerge not merely as a brilliant inspiration, but as a skilful piece of structure, rich in invention but sturdily unified in style and composition, full of melody but rich in polyphony, richer, indeed, in counterpoint than any other Verdi opera. Through the way in which its structures translate dramatic conflict into thoroughly organised musical discourses — total music leaving no space for recitative or declamation, almost wholly absorbed into continuous action by way of musical logic — we can ask ourselves whether *Il Trovatore* may not be styled Verdi's most *Mozartian* opera.

*

But how was *Il Trovatore* conceived?

We do not know for certain how and when Verdi came across Garcia

* from 'atti dell III° Congresso internazionale di studi verdiani' held in Milan, 1972, and published in Parma 1974.

8

Theodor Wachtel as Manrico (Theatre Museum)

Mme Lemaire one of the first to sing Azucena in London (Theatre Museum)

Gutiérrez's play *El trovador*, but it is likely that in January or February of 1851, during the most unsettled period of composition and rehearsal of *Rigoletto* and his difficulties over that work with the Venetian censor, the composer obtained a translation of the Spanish play and sent it to the Neapolitan poet Salvatore Cammarano. On March 29, 1851, less than twenty days before *Rigoletto*'s première, Verdi requested, through his friend De Sanctis, a reply from Cammarano as to *Il Trovatore*, warning that 'the more he offers me something novel and unconventional, the better I'll do'. The history of *Trovatore*'s creation thus occupies a two-year period, from early 1851 until January 1853, coinciding, in its last months, with the creation of *La Traviata* (which was to appear in Venice a few weeks after the première of *Il Trovatore*).

These two years were marked by several significant events in Verdi's life: his mother's death, on June 28, 1851, and that of Cammarano himself on July 17, 1852; a stay in Paris with Giuseppina from mid-December, 1851, to mid-March, 1852; his nomination as a Chevalier de la Légion d'Honneur in August, 1852; numerous theatrical projects and the signing of two important contracts: one on February 28, 1852, with the Paris Opéra (for *Les Vêpres Siciliennes*) the other on May 4, 1852, with La Fenice, Venice (for what was to be *La Traviata*) followed in the June of that year by the contract for *Trovatore* in Rome with the impresario Jacovacci. Contrary to his usual habits, Verdi launched the project before he had fixed terms with an impresario or with publishers. There was merely a vague agreement with Cammarano, to whom, in September, 1849, he had originally suggested *Le Roi s'amuse*. When the librettist expressed anxiety on this subject, foreseeing problems with the censor, Verdi replaced Hugo's drama (which he had then passed on to Piave) with Shakespeare's *King Lear*. Doubly preoccupied, however, with *Stiffelio* and *Rigoletto*, Verdi himself later asked Cammarano to put *King Lear* aside until they could deal with such a tough assignment in an atmosphere of greater calm and concentration.

In the programme of collaboration which Verdi proposed to Cammarano without contractual obligations to managers or publishers, *Trovatore* in one sense took the place of the *King Lear* project. After the retirement of Felice Romani, Cammarano was considered the most prestigious of Italian librettists. For his part Verdi held him in the sort of sincere esteem he showed none of his other theatre poets, except possibly Boito; his admiration was confirmed by a continued collaboration ended only by the poet's unexpected death. Cammarano had already written the texts of *Alzira* (1845), *La Battaglia di Legnano* (1849) and *Luisa Miller* (1849) for Verdi. Less inspired than Solera, less bold than Piave with the composer's spur behind him, but far more expert in theatrical matters and the finer versifier, Cammarano distinguished himself by librettos with neatly constructed plots and lucid dialogue. It was his usual practice to present his characters one at a time (hence the sequence of cavatinas which open each libretto) to establish each individually and to develop the action so as to achieve a gradual rise in dramatic tension. Never at a loss for poetic images, he knew how to capture the mood of a situation in a single opening verse. Lines like *'Verranno a te sull'aure'* and *'Cruda, funesta smania'* from *Lucia di Lammermoor* or *'D'amor sull'ali rosee' (No. 12* in *Trovatore*), and many others, have become almost proverbial in Italian not just because of their memorable melodies but because of their evocative power.

Above all Cammarano had the unusual gift of not restricting himself to a libretto's purely literary aspects: few Italian librettists after Metastasio, and none after Cammarano (except Boito), were so much aware of the need to offer a composer the sort of scenic and verbal structure which could naturally be translated into musical terms, and which allowed him to construct complete musical numbers from the sequence of scenes. Cammarano wrote librettos while thinking of music. In 1849, during work on *Luisa Miller*, he had written to Verdi:

> If I were not afraid of being called Utopian, I should be tempted to say that to reach perfection in a musical work a single mind should create the verses and the music: on this premise I base my opinion that if there are to be two creators, they must at least fraternise, and that if Poetry must not be Music's servant, then neither must it become its tyrant. I have always worked according to this principle, of which I am convinced, and have always placed this aim before those composers with whom I have shared my task.

Used to a concept of opera that was developed from 1835 onwards by composers like Mercadante and Donizetti, Cammarano in *Il Trovatore* faced a Verdi committed to 'the boldest possible subjects, clad in the newest forms', a Verdi whose energies seemed redoubled, and whose imagination had been unleashed, by the labours of *Rigoletto* — most decidedly 'a daring subject clad in a new form'. An eloquent testimony to this creative phase in the composer's life is the letter in which he replied, on April 24, 1851, to the poet's objections about the adaptation of *Trovatore*:

> . . . You do not say a word as to whether you like the play. I suggested it to you because it seems to me to offer excellent dramatic features and, in addition, something singular and original . . . As to the distribution of the numbers, I tell you that when somebody sends me poetry to set to music, every form and distribution is appropriate, though the newer and more bizarre they are, the happier I am. If there were no Cavatinas, Duets, Trios, Choruses, Finales etc. etc., in operas, I should find this more reasonable and right. So I tell you that if you can avoid an opening

Gwyneth Jones as Leonora at Covent
Garden in 1964 (photo: Donald Southern)

Ladislaus Konya as the Count at Covent
Garden in 1973 (photo: Donald Southern)

chorus (every opera starts with an opening chorus) and a cavatina for
Leonora, and begin directly with the Troubadour's song and make a
single act from the first two, then this would be splendid, since such
pieces isolated by scene changes seem more like items in a concert than
an opera. If you can, please do it . . . As to the rest do as you think best.
When one has a Cammarano, one can hardly go far wrong.

Yet, because the subject demanded it, the result was an opera that has an
introductory scene with chorus and, indeed, cavatinas, duets, trios, choruses
and finales. For many commentators this formal structure seems to be a
retreat from the novelties of *Rigoletto*, novelties allowed and to a certain
extent determined by Hugo's conception of rapid and straightforward action.
In fact *Il Trovatore* is an appreciable advance: Verdi, with his markedly
dialectic notions of form, knew how to enclose the complex, two-pronged plot
structure (Manrico-Leonora-Count, Manrico-Azucena-Count) in a score
with a clearly organised musical argument. A precise selection of tonal
relationships and sound pictures conveys each scene within this overall
conception.

An eloquent example of the dialectic that heightens these dramatic conflicts
appears in the new scenario sent by Verdi to Cammarano on April 9, 1851:

> I have read your scenario, and, being a man of talent and superior
> character, you will hardly be offended if so wretched a creature as
> myself takes the liberty to tell you that if this subject, on our stage,
> cannot incorporate all the freshness and strangeness of the Spanish
> play, it would be better to give it up. I may be wrong, but it seems as
> though several of the situations have lost their earlier force and
> originality, and that Azucena particularly lacks her essential strangeness
> and novelty of character; it seems as though this woman's two great
> passions [filial and maternal love] no longer figure at their most
> powerful . . . I should not wish Azucena to tell her tale to the gipsies or

for her to go mad at the end. I want you to leave in the great Aria!! Eleonora has no part in the Song of the Dead and the Troubadour's Air, and this seems to me one of the best positions for an aria.

From this we can deduce that Verdi was already contemplating the great *Miserere* scene, one of the finest and most original inspirations of romantic opera. And just as in *Rigoletto* he had picked out, in a flash of theatrical intuition, the curse as the driving force behind the drama, in *Trovatore* Verdi fixed upon a similar idea in the gipsy's *vengeance*, underlined in his letter to Cammarano on April 4: 'the last words of the drama are *'Sei vendicata'* ('you are avenged).' He confirmed this on April 9: 'we must preserve till the very last this woman's two great passions: her love for Manrique and her burning thirst to avenge her mother's death.'

Preparation of the libretto proceeded calmly, as had seldom been the case with Verdi's earlier texts: the composer imposed no obligations whatever. But on September 9, 1851, he once more started urging the poet:

A host of serious matters has prevented me hitherto from thinking sincerely about *Il Trovatore*. Now that I can recover breath a little, however, I must concern myself once again with my art and my affairs. Rome and Venice have asked me for operas . . . The Rome company is better adapted to *Il Trovatore*, but someone is lacking to take the role of Azucena, that Azucena by whom I set such store!

While Verdi began negotiations for the performance of *Trovatore*, of which he had not composed a single note (even if, as we may suppose, he had the *tinta musicale* — musical colouring — worked out) the unexpected news arrived in February, 1852, of Cammarano's illness. From Paris the composer wrote to De Sanctis:

This delay in finishing *Trovatore* has been decidedly prejudicial to me. I have refused a whole heap of contracts, and I could have given the piece here with an excellent company, if only the libretto were finished. But never mind! Let's not think of the past.

Despite Cammarano's illness preparation of the text went ahead, however slowly, and in June Verdi confirmed his readiness to give the opera in Rome. But on July 17, when the libretto seemed nearly ready, Cammarano died. Verdi expressed a genuine grief to De Sanctis: 'I was struck as though by lightning at the sad news of Cammarano's death. It is impossible to describe my profound sadness to you!' But the Roman engagement was already confirmed; only the censor's approval of the text was required. Verdi charged Emmanuele Bardare, Cammarano's pupil, with all the necessary cuts and possible adjustments. In September (as we can see from the composer's letter to his publisher Ricordi, thanking him for sending music paper) Verdi started composing, and on December 14 he could already tell the Roman sculptor Luccardi that '*Il Trovatore* is completely finished, down to the very last note, and I'm pleased with it. As long as the Romans are too! . . .' Six days later he set off for Rome, to finish (as was his custom) the orchestration during rehearsals: he took the libretto of *La Traviata* with him.

On the eve of the first performance of *Trovatore*, at the Teatro di Apollo on January 19, 1853, the Tiber burst its banks flooding the low-lying quarter of the city where the theatre stood. Perhaps it may be seen as a symbol of the deluge caused by the opera as it flooded European stages with its melodies, and swept, after only a few years, over the remotest corners of five continents. In April it was already being given at Ancona, in May at Ferrara and Reggio

Bruno Prevedi (Manrico) and Giulietta Simionato (Azucena) at Covent Garden in 1964 (photo: Donald Southern)

Emilia; in June it triumphed at Forli, at Padua and at Faenza, in July at Vicenza and Siena, in August at Bergamo and Livorno, in September at Fermo, Corfu, Urbino and at La Scala, Milan; in the autumn it fired audiences in Malta, Bologna, Florence, Naples, Trieste, Palermo, Rovigo, Constantinople, Ascoli and Messina; finally, on Boxing Day it opened the carnival season at Genoa, Mantua, Modena, Venice and Verona: in a single year thirty different theatres had thus given Verdi's new opera. The following year the figure was more than doubled: over 65 theatres gave their first *Trovatore* (this does not include repeat performances), and over 70 more in 1855. On Boxing Day, 1854, some fifteen theatres mounted their first *Trovatore*, which means that less than two years after the *prima assoluta* at least fifteen Manricos and as many Leonoras, Azucenas and Count di Lunas could be produced ... and at the same time there was a need to increase production of a new musical instrument required by the score — the anvil.

It was not just a success, it was a fashion. At the end of 1853, the Neapolitan comedian Pasquale Altavilla*, put on at the San Carlino theatre his three-act comedy *Na Famiglia ntusiasmata pe la museca de lo Trovatore* (*A family wild for the music of 'Il Trovatore'*): its popularity lasted well into this century. Ricordi brought an ill-fated lawsuit in 1883 against the *pulcinella* De Martino, when he revived it in Rome, but lost the case. Altogether different was Verdi's own attitude: a keen enthusiast for the Milanese actor Edoardo Ferravilla, he went with Boito to see him perform *Minestron*, a parody of *Trovatore*, and kept as souvenirs on his writing desk two grotesque statues of Ferravilla and Giraud in costume.

A deluge indeed. In 1854 *Il Trovatore* was given from Madrid to Odessa, from Warsaw to Rio de Janeiro; in 1855 in Buenos Aires and Bucharest, Alexandria and London (on May 10 at Covent Garden, with Enrico Tamberlick, Francesco Graziani, Jenny Ney and Pauline Viardot Garcia, conducted by Sir Michael Costa), and in Liverpool, St Petersburg and the Balearics. In 1856 it reached Edinburgh and Moscow, Recife and Mexico, while in London it was given in English (Drury Lane, March 14); in 1858 at Lvov; in 1859 at San Francisco, Smyrna, Riga and in Australia; in 1860 in Sweden, Algeria and Guatemala; in 1862 at Saint Thomas in the West Indies; in 1864 at Kharkov, Bombay and in Costa Rica; in 1866 at Calcutta and the Sandwich Islands; in 1868 in the Philippines, and thus it went on ...

So Verdi could justly, if jokingly, write to his friend Arrivabene in May 1862: 'When you go to India and to the interior of Africa you'll hear *Trovatore.*' Such an inundation must even have penetrated to the apparently musically insensitive ears of Cavour, who received, on April 23, 1859, the ultimatum from Austria which was to bring in France on the side of Piedmont in the war of Italian Unity. Incapable of putting his accumulated excitement into words, he started waving the despatch about and flung the window open to sing *'Di quella pira'* at the top of his voice ...

Few operas have enjoyed such widespread and immediate popularity, or have so solidly established themselves in the fabric of social history. Its part in such a history is inscribed on the spear-point of that famous *'o teco'* in *'Di quella pira'* — that high C which Verdi never wrote but accepted in deference to the golden rule of varying the repeats in a *rondò* or a *cabaletta*. All too often it decides the fate of a performance: it is an awful, unavoidable assignment which no tenor knows how to renounce — a glimmering flash in which all the revolutionary spirit of *Il Trovatore* seems to be condensed. Preserved on hundreds of records (one American company a few years ago had the idea of bringing together on a single disc the forty best recorded renderings!), it is enshrined in the famous opening sequence of Visconti's film *Senso*, in which the aria is the signal for a Risorgimento riot at the Fenice opera house in Venice. The story of this opera is that of the singers who have scaled the vault of gravity-defying melodies in the 'Via Crucis of Italian song'. It is also a story of the audiences all over the world who have understood Verdi's intentions in *Trovatore* a century before any musicological studies of them.

---

* His lucky career had been eulogised by Filippo Cammarano, uncle of the librettist and author of a farce entitled *Li Contraste tra duje Mpressarie pe li mmuseche de li Maste Verdi e Donizetti* (*The Quarrels between two Impresarios over the music of Verdi and Donizetti*).

'Il Trovatore': Music and Drama

D.R.B. Kimbell

Some forty years ago E.J. Dent remarked that when he told his friends he was translating *Il Trovatore*, they looked at him rather as they might have done 'if I had announced the birth of a bastard baby'. One reason why fastidious critics viewed the opera with disdain was certainly its grotesque plot; another was the fact that it was a last relic of the discredited Italian melodramatic tradition of the early nineteenth century, the tradition swept away not only by the avowedly hostile Wagner, but by Verdi himself in his later works. The old-fashioned character of the opera was shown in its dependence upon closed musical forms; in the way it upheld the supremacy of the singing voice, and neglected, comparatively speaking, the favourite expressive resources of the Romantic age: richly-coloured orchestration, chromaticism and dissonance.

Il Trovatore certainly acknowledges its traditionalism far more frankly than do the nearly contemporary *Rigoletto* and *La Traviata*. But that is not the result of a mere lapse into indolence on Verdi's part: it reflects the character of the drama he is setting. Traditional formalism would not have done for a subtly developing psychological drama such as *La Traviata*; but *Il Trovatore* deals in the conflicts of elemental passion, and for that the song-based structures of traditional opera are ideal. We find in unique abundance picturesque choruses, dramatic ensembles ablaze with conflict, impassioned arias steeped in intense, almost exotic melancholy. But any danger that the opera might become statuesque as a result of all these set-pieces is averted, partly by the dynamism of the passages which link them together, partly by the new style of lyrical movement which Verdi had mastered by the 1850s. He builds them up — whether slow or fast — with a gradually gathering momentum, so that they reach their climax and fulfilment only in the final phrases.

Thanks to its ardent lyricism and unflagging theatrical verve, *Il Trovatore* is as thrilling today as it was for the audiences that first acclaimed it in Rome in 1853. And the connoisseur now acknowledges what was always obvious to the plain opera-goer; *Il Trovatore*, once beyond the pale of cultivated taste, is admired as one of the greatest of Verdi's works.

A note on terminology

Most of the numbers of *Il Trovatore* are composed in the multisectional form that Rossini had established a generation earlier. Its constituent parts were as follows:

i   instrumental prelude — normally found only when the number has been preceded by a change of scene.

ii   recitative or *scena* — the term *scena* implies a more varied and fully-composed scene, perhaps with sections of lyrical writing or a fuller role for the orchestra than in a simple recitative.

iii   *primo tempo* — only used in ensemble scenes; often declamatory in style, and with its momentum supplied by the orchestra. It 'sets up' the following *cantabile*.

iv   *cantabile* — the lyrical heart of the scene: normally a slow and reflective aria.

v   *tempo di mezzo* — the transition, or linking passage which effects the shift of mood between the *cantabile* and the other main aria section, the *cabaletta*.

vi   *cabaletta* or *stretta* — the term *stretta* is often preferred in ensembles for more than two singers. Normally a fast and brilliant aria sung twice.

15

Before the curtain rises

Two strands run through the plot, each attached to one of the female principals. Azucena, the gipsy, is the daughter of a woman who some twenty years before has been burnt for witchcraft — she was thought to have cast an evil eye on the infant son of a Spanish nobleman. In a vengeful frenzy Azucena intended to throw this baby on the embers of the pyre, but, in her distraction, she burnt her own baby son instead. Ever since she has been haunted by apparitions of her mother calling for vengeance. The romantic heroine is Leonora, a lady at the Aragonese Court; she is loved by both the Count di Luna, a grandee of the Kingdom, and by Manrico. He, a 'troubadour', is an outlaw in the civil war which is raging, but it is he who has won Leonora's heart. These rivals, Luna and Manrico, are the means by which the two strands of plot become tangled together. Luna is the son of the count who had the gipsy burnt, and still hopes one day to find the gipsy and avenge the supposed death of his brother. Manrico has been brought up by Azucena among the gipsies as her son. In fact, he is the child she had intended to burn, and therefore Luna's younger brother!

Part One: The Duel

The Count passes whole nights sighing beneath Leonora's balcony. One such night, while awaiting his return, Ferrando tells Luna's retainers and men-at-arms the story of Azucena and her mother; they exchange rumours about the ghostly forms in which the hag continues to appear. Meanwhile, in the palace, Leonora confides in her companion Inez: an unknown knight won her love by his bravery at a tourney in the days before the civil war: since then he has sometimes returned in the guise of a troubadour. Through the garden, first Luna, and then Manrico, approach. Leonora descends to greet Manrico and blunders into the arms of Luna. A scene of confrontation ends the act: Luna, already madly jealous to find a troubadour preferred to himself, is stung to greater fury when his rival reveals himself as the rebel Manrico. The men rush away to duel.

No. 1 Introduction

The opening pages have all the economy and pace that is to typify the whole opera. There is no formal overture or prelude, but with a few bars of drum rolls, fanfares, and soft horn-calls, Verdi at once transports us into a world of romance and chivalry. That there are three narrative arias in the opening scenes indicates the important role that the past plays in the drama. Memories of past events are nursed with the deepest emotions and the characters identify with the stories so strongly as to bring them to life. Ferrando's *'Di due figli'* ('Heaven had given') is the first of these arias. Each of its two verses falls into two parts. The first and shorter — *andante mosso*, eerily coloured by low clarinets and bassoons — employs a great deal of bare octave writing in declamatory style, partly to help the singer project the words clearly, partly to give the music an introductory character so that the expressive weight of the narration falls on the following *allegretto* section. For besides continuing the tale of horror this *allegretto* has a second crucial function: Azucena may not appear until Part Two of the opera, but she is the motivating force of the whole drama, and this is a musical evocation of her world of gipsy witchcraft. It is in 'her' key of E minor; and with its triple rhythm, its strumming waltz-like accompaniment, and its square-cut repetitive phrasing, it has the primitive *popolaresco* tone that will be heard in her music throughout the opera.

The introduction closes with the stretta *'Sull'orlo dei tetti'*('Up there on the roof top') [2], a remarkable piece of tone-painting shared between Ferrando and the chorus but in unison virtually throughout, and to be played 'extremely softly'. As the men describe the subhuman reincarnations in which the dead gipsy appears, the music flits past as if propelled by bats' wings. It ends with an astonishing *coup-de-théâtre*: the ghostings the chorus describe bring the story of Azucena's mother slowly into the present, and as they remember an old retainer who was struck dead with horror when he was visited by the ghost one midnight, it does indeed strike midnight. The men scream with terror, and the *pianissimo* is swept away in one of those great Verdian outbursts which in one mighty phrase discharge the pent-up emotions of the whole scene.

No. 2 Cavatina

A short instrumental prelude introduces the most eagerly awaited number in a romantic Italian opera, the entrance aria (that is the 19th-century significance of the term 'cavatina') of the *prima donna*: it will be particularly savoured when the opening scene has been for male voices only.

The recitative — to describe simply one of many similar examples in the opera — shows the incomparable precision with which Verdi always highlights the primary expressive and dramatic issues. After nearly five bars of unaccompanied singing he places the first string chord to point the yearning melancholy of Leonora's *'Un altra notte ancora senza vederlo'* ('Another night will pass and I shall not see him'); traditional devices of accompanied recitative — tremolo and dotted rhythms — give weight to Leonora's account of her first meeting with Manrico at the lists. The real point of the scene is not story-telling, however, but the depiction of Leonora's dawning love, and the recitative closes with an exquisite *arioso* supported by trilling violin and gently floating *arpeggios* on flute and clarinet to express this: the memory of Manrico is 'like some golden vision seen in [her] slumbers!'

Unlike the recitative, the two-verse *cantabile 'Tacea la notte'* ('The stars shone in the heavens') [3], is not concerned with precise analogies between text and music. Whatever the details of Cammarano's text, the aria expresses in incomparably eloquent lyrical music the flowering of Leonora's love. From its quiet scene-setting opening, this flowering is expressed in a shift from the melancholy minor key, via various related keys, to the rapturous major key of the close, and in a melody which slowly rises in pitch to climax in a towering cadence phrase, laden with *appoggiaturas* and given an extra thrill by the chromatically rising inner voice of cellos and bassoon. The second verse is enriched by variation: by touches of *parlando* to recapture the excitement of *'un nome ... il nome mio'* ('a name repeated ... it was my own') and *'egli era! ... egli era desso'* ('I saw him, saw him beside me'), and, especially, by the

Rita Hunter as Leonora at ENO (photo: John Garner)

repetition, expansion and enrichment of the final great phrase. Notice the breath-holding stillness at the start of the repeat, and then — a frequent feature of Verdi's most ecstatic lyricism — the dissolution of every rhythmic feature into a shimmer of background harmonies.

The scene closes with a brilliant *cabaletta*, *'Di tale amor'* ('No words can tell') [4], the only aria in the opera with a formal introduction. It would be a mistake to regard its sparkling virtuosity simply as a recipe for stopping the show — though it should surely do that! More importantly the array of *coloratura* devices, the breath-catching semiquaver rests, the trills and glides, are the musical vocabulary of giddy intoxicated rapture.

No. 3 Scena, Romance and Terzet

Another prelude depicts the approach of the Count, softly and smoothly, yet with a wealth of chromatic detail to suggest his inner perturbation. Again the recitative is masterly, whispered into the silences, an accompaniment added only when the time comes to give expressive weight to his yearning, and culminating in a glorious *arioso* phrase of which even Verdi's greatest lovers would not be ashamed. Let Luna's first scene be remembered. For he is no merely conventional villain: first and foremost he is a lover, as ardent and nearly as youthful as Manrico himself, and it is the unendurable frustration of his love that drives him to treachery and brutality.

As Luna approaches the palace, the sounds of a harp float across the garden through the darkness. It is Manrico, the troubadour, and his *romanza 'Deserto sulla terra'* ('Though nought on earth is left me') [5] — which is not, of course, designed to wake everyone in the palace, but should be sung in a mysterious *mezza voce* — is the lyrical heart of this scene. Verdi exploits this *coup-de-théâtre* magnificently. It is music from the same melancholy, extravagantly romantic gipsy world that we have already heard described in Ferrando's aria: strophic form, triple rhythm, balladesque harp accompaniment, minor key harmonies with touches of modality.

The following *allegro*, in which the greater part of the action is concentrated, is one of the best examples in the opera of the so-called *parlante* style, in which the declamation of the text is carried along on the momentum of a continuously developing orchestral theme. It will be noticed how these developments reflect the mood of the characters: at first sorrowful and breathless, to match Leonora's agitated distress; then veering from key to key as the tension builds up between the rival lovers; finally thundering in the bass as they square up for the duel.

In the stretta *'Di geloso amor'* ('Jealous fury') [6], Cammarano had given each of the three characters a complete verse to sing. It is typical of Verdi's radical theatricality that he should reduce this rational symmetry to a stark confrontation of Luna *versus* Leonora and Manrico, singing together in octaves. However this may impair the audibility of the text, it has the great merit of embodying the situation in instantly intelligible musical terms. So fiercely do the passions rage that the accompaniment has no time for the articulation of distinct figures and is reduced to a hectic pounding of chords. In the second statement Luna's solo is shortened: it breaks down into a muttering theme, which continues as a menacing undercurrent to the lovers' song.

Part Two: The Gipsy

A year of civil war has passed. Manrico defeated Luna in the duel, but spared his life. He in turn has been grievously injured by Luna in battle and has been nursed back to health by Azucena. As the gipsies prepare for their day's work Azucena sings a ballad about a woman who was burnt at the stake. The theatre audience will appreciate that this is the story of her own mother, but Manrico is mystified and, when he hears Azucena muttering 'Avenge me!', perturbed. After the gipsies have left, he asks her to tell him more; which she does, describing in full detail her mother's horrific death and her own ill-fated attempt at vengeance. Then she regrets revealing so much and tries to reassure Manrico: of course he is her son; what she said was muddled because the memory of her mother confuses her mind. Their talk turns to Luna. Why ever did Manrico spare the life of the man she longs to destroy? He is unable to explain the sudden impulse to mercy that overcame him as Luna lay defenceless before him. A messenger brings Manrico a commission from the rebel prince, Urgel; also the news that Leonora, believing the troubadour dead, is about to take the veil. Sweeping aside all Azucena's objections, Manrico hastily departs.

Luna too has heard of Leonora's plan, and outside the nunnery organises his men to abduct her. Having, as he supposes, rid himself of Manrico, he must now snatch her from the arms of a heavenly rival. As Leonora bids farewell to Inez and her attendants, Luna steps out of the shadows. But he in turn is confounded by the intervention of Manrico, who, with the aid of his followers, hurries Leonora away.

No. 4 Chorus of gipsies and Canzona

The chorus provides a frame for Azucena's *canzona* but is not intrinsically more than a picturesque scene-setter. Verdi has packed a profusion of characteristic detail into the orchestral writing — the exotic percussion effects include triangle and anvils added to the usual timpani and bass-drum; and there are trills, and stabbing and sliding grace-notes, of a kind we have already begun to associate with the gipsy milieu. As so often in *Il Trovatore*, the lyrical climax comes at the close, in the well-loved unison theme sung against the clashing of the anvils, and it is this memorable phrase that periodically recurs to give audible shape to what might otherwise have been a desultory sort of scene.

It was Verdi's own idea to introduce Azucena's *canzona* here. A *canzona* is a song within the opera — a movement that would be sung even if the rest of the drama were spoken, and it is modelled on the song which García Gutiérrez himself incorporated into *El trovador* at this juncture (see p. 00). It is not to be understood therefore as a spontaneous expression of Azucena's feelings: her mother's fate has been transmuted into legend and is remembered in the form

The 1947 Covent Garden production designed by Derek Hill

of a folk-ballad. Verdi himself emphasized the *canzona*'s 'popular' character, and designed it with a view to having it recur from time to time as a musical analogy to Azucena's recurring obsession with revenge. The music is again in Azucena's E minor and again in triple time: reiterated rhythms, obsessive repeated notes, shuddering trills, and starkly contrasted dynamics give it a bizarre vehemence.

No. 5 Scena and Racconto
Azucena's *'Condotta ell' era in ceppi'* ('They brought her, fettered and powerless') [11] is her version of the story told by Ferrando in Part One. Consequently the preliminary details, so lavishly recorded by Ferrando, are passed over, to concentrate on Azucena's compassion for her mother, and on the bestiality of her persecutors. Surely both these features are suggested in the orchestral textures accompanying the aria, which is in Verdi's richest and most expressively pointed style: whereas many of the *Trovatore* accompaniments are of a simple pulsing or dancing kind, here the reiterated chords are enriched with stabbingly accentuated tremors from the inner strings and a sighing figure in oboe and first violin. Are these perhaps musical similes, the one for the whip lashes inflicted on the wretched victim, the other for her lamentations?

While the previous narrative arias have been stanzaic, this one breaks down under the strain of Azucena's emotion: she is not simply telling a story, but reliving the most appalling experience of her life. What began as a regularly-structured aria, saturated with the peculiar *Trovatore* melancholy and crammed with expressive touches from the orchestra, develops into a whole series of contrasting paragraphs, each taking its style from the incident which for the moment haunts Azucena's memory: the whimpering of the baby boy she intended to burn; the apparition of her mother's ghost; the delirium in which she tossed the wrong child into the flames; her final emotional prostration. It was for the periodic apparitions of the ghost that Verdi wanted an evocative and easily identifiable recurring theme, and that section of the narrative provides the pretext for a first restatement of *'Stride la vampa'* ('Fierce flames are raging') [10], high up on tremolo strings.

No. 6 Scena and Duet
So far we have heard Manrico in the roles of lover, knight and troubadour. This scene concentrates on his tender relationship with Azucena and the mysterious impulse of compassion that overcame him when he had Luna at his mercy. In the long and rather confusing recitative with which Cammarano prefaces the duet, these are precisely the motifs that Verdi emphasises. The following *cantabile 'Mal reggendo all'aspro assalto'* ('As we struggled he stumbled before me') [12], continues to explore the reactions of Manrico and Azucena to the duel fought so many months ago. Again the narrative element is pronounced, and a salient musical characteristic is the care with which Verdi projects the text.

After the delivery of the letter, tension mounts steeply in the *parlante* leading into *'Perigliarti ancor languente'* ('You are still too weak to venture') [14], a *cabaletta* of conflict. Azucena's verse begins with mere old-womanly agitation but develops into the most ardent expression yet of her maternal love; it closes, astonishingly, with a *cadenza*. The purpose of this is not simply to show off the singer's high notes, but to express Azucena's determination that she is saying the last word on Manrico's fitness to chase off after Leonora. But the music with which the hero counters is irresistible [15]: its major key, its immovable stamping tonic pedal, the sharper vigour of its rhythm sweep aside all Azucena's objections.

The last pages of the movement provide in a nutshell a nice lesson in Verdian aesthetics. Having vividly depicted the characters in conflict in contrasting paragraphs of song, he allows them to join in ecstatic unison. Ultimately the lyricism of Italian opera rises above a mere evocation of the characters' feelings, into a state of exultation that is not limited to any particular dramatic or expressive purpose. But Verdi punctuates such lyrical raptures with reminders of the dramatic issue out of which they arose: at 'Ferma, deh! ferma! — Mi lascia, mi lascia . . .' a sudden plunge into the minor and a new rapping figure in the orchestra brings the conflict back into focus.

No. 7 Scena and Aria

As Luna's first *scena* was that of a lover, so now with his first aria: indeed *'Il balen del suo sorriso'* ('All the stars that shine above me') [16] is one of Verdi's greatest love-songs, and must give further pause to anyone supposing the count to be merely villainous. Much of the music heard so far in *Il Trovatore* has been in a rather squarely reiterative popular style. *'Il balen'* is in Verdi's most aristocratic manner, its phrases gradually unfolded, and adorned by Luna more and more tenderly. Initially the song is exquisitely tuned to the dramatic context, pitched rather low and with dark-hued scoring — chalumeau clarinets, violas, cellos, basses, with touches of bassoon and horn to warm the cadences. But, of course, Verdi does not attempt to sustain this naturalism; no small part of the ardour of the closing phrases is due to the addition of violins, flutes and oboes to Luna's song, now pitched at the very top of the baritone range. After the stillness of the opening the swaying rhythm of the accompaniment and the regular swing of the harmonies add their part to the paean of love.

If *'Il balen'* is one of the most admired numbers in the opera, its *cabaletta*, *'Per me ora fatale'* ('My hour of joy approaches') [18], is one of the most easily mocked. The element that has been most often parodied, the framing chorus, which for minutes on end sings 'We'll hide away . . . no more delay!', was added to the original *cabaletta* text at Verdi's express request. For modern audiences the scene has been made more than ever difficult to swallow as a result of the fashion for quasi-realistic production. But the arias and ensembles of Italian opera — of *Il Trovatore* more perhaps than most — tend to catch the characters in a deeply-experienced moment and then suspend time: they are closer to Keats's *Grecian Urn* than to cinematography. The

Act Two in John Copley's ENO production designed by Stefanos Lazaridis with Norman Bailey, Jon Sydney and Rita Hunter (photo: Anthony Crickmay)

challenge for producer and audience alike is to experience the aria whole — the count raging with passion, the retainers nervously in hiding — and not to let the antithesis and alternation of stentorian lyricism and whispered snippets of patter imply that time is passing realistically.

No. 8 Second Finale

Much of the finale too is a tableau in sound, and while the opening bars are given over largely to a nuns' chorus, we are not allowed to forget that there are ruffians lurking in the bushes. The scene begins to come to life in the dialogue between Leonora and Inez that follows: starting unaccompanied, playing a single string chord when it helps Leonora to speak her sorrow most eloquently, and culminating in an exquisitely poignant *arioso*, this quietly meditative episode is the lull before the storm of events that sweeps into the main part of the ensemble, the *andante mosso, 'E degg'io e posso'* ('Oh can it be') [20].

This is basically a trio, though eventually it involves the full complement of singers. Leonora sings first — her whole verse of text, in setting which Verdi aims in masterly, confident fashion at the clinching lines:

Have you come down from Heaven,	Sei tu dal ciel disceso
Or am I there by your side?	O in ciel son io con te.

Breathlessness, astonishment, enchantment are evoked by wisps of melody, tentatively sketched harmonies, rhythms that at once dance and gasp. In the culminating phrase the whispered dynamics and surprised rhythms are at first retained but the melody is more sustained, the harmonies fuller, and it mounts tremendously to its peak before pouring itself out into the cadence. While Leonora is in an enraptured world of her own, the two men confront one another: their verses are broken up into smaller units and hurled defiantly backwards and forwards. Manrico adopts Luna's hectoring manner but has additional resources of tessitura and rhythmic virtuosity to draw upon. After this 'exposition', all dramatic verisimilitude is abandoned: the frozen tableau on stage has its musical counterpart in a richly detailed pattern extended into a beautifully symmetrical form. Leonora, the most distinctive lyrical personality, resumes the panting style of her solo verse; Manrico cuts through the vocal mass from time to time with soaring *cantabile* phrases; everyone else is merged into the rich but anonymous tapestry of sound.

The act ends with a rapid series of violent incidents, all embodied in the music. But operatically more to the point is that we should carry with us the memory of the crowning emotional experience of the finale. This effect is achieved by a sudden freeze, during which the glorious culminating theme from Leonora's solo — *'Sei tu dal ciel disceso'* — returns transfigured, against shimmering string harmonies.

Act Two at Covent Garden in 1981 with Joan Sutherland, Franco Bonisolli and Yuri Masurok (photo: Reg Wilson)

Part Three: The Gipsy's Son

The third act of *Il Trovatore* is the one part of the opera in which the spectator is keenly aware of the background of civil war, so important in the play. The Count di Luna and his soldiers are encamped a few miles from the rebel stronghold held by Manrico, and are preparing for the assault. Stronger than any political consideration in Luna's mind is his jealous determination to tear Leonora from the arms of his rival. Some soldiers drag in a gipsy who has been arrested on suspicion of spying. During the interrogation, Ferrando recognizes her as Azucena, and in her terror she calls out for Manrico. Luna's exultation knows no bounds: by burning the gipsy before the walls of the beleaguered fortress he can torment his rival at the same time as avenging the death of his supposed brother.

Meanwhile Manrico and Leonora are about to be married. Ruiz reports that a pyre is being erected outside the walls, and that Azucena is being led towards it in chains. With a hasty explanation to the confounded Leonora, Manrico leads off his men to attempt a rescue.

No. 9 Introductory Chorus

A fine specimen of the traditional scene-setting chorus: nothing more than a picture in sound of the bustling activity and soaring spirits in camp before an eagerly anticipated battle. Its central portion *'Squilli, echeggi la tromba guerriera'* ('Let all the trumpets set echoes replying') [22], has a rhythmic verve unprecedented in Verdi's choruses – perhaps a reflection of his experience of Meyerbeer's music in Paris.

No. 10 Scena and Terzet

It had been the librettist's intention to start this scene with a recitative and *romanza* for Luna. And while the *romanza* was abandoned when *'Il balen'* was added to Part Two, it is good that the passionate recitative remains; it helps remind us that Luna's moral decline is hastened by the emotional frustrations with which he is continually beset. In Part One he confronted his adversary as a man of honour; in Part Two he was driven to sacrilege; now romantic jealousy brings out an ugly streak of sadistic cruelty. Although describing the scene as a terzet, Verdi has actually set the *cantabile* as a solo for Azucena, and the *cabaletta* as an Azucena/Luna duet to which Ferrando, and the chorus, contribute only in the most subsidiary capacity.

In its progression from balladesque minor to impassioned major, the short aria *'Giorni poveri vivea'* ('Though my life was poor') [23] depicts the whole range of Azucena's character, from naive simplicity to passionate motherhood. By eliminating from the accompaniment all strongly rhythmic features and all incidental touches of colour Verdi concentrates the expression almost entirely in the singing voice. The continuous reverberation of the tonic chord — E minor again! — in the opening bars endows the music with all the elemental melancholy so typical of *Il Trovatore*. When the first fleeting glimpses of the major key sink back into the minor, we feel it to be a perfect lyrical analogy to the words:

| But alas! my son has left me | Sola speme un figlio avea |
| All alone and unprotected. | Mi lascio . . . mi obblia, l'ingrato |

and we notice again how closely some of Verdi's finest melodies are inspired by their texts. Throughout the song, the woodwind instruments are used almost as if they were an embodiment of Azucena's vision of Manrico, making warm and sonorous the music of the central G major section, and joining Azucena's melody as it tugs with *appoggiaturas* at the cadential harmonies in the climactic phrase:

Fonder love than I still bear him,	Qual per esso provo amore
No mother here on earth could show.	Madre in terra non provo!

Because it is the aria that deepens the suspicion of her interrogators, there is no break at the end of it: instead the *tempo di mezzo* is propelled on a lyrical orchestral theme that is heard as its natural continuation.

The *cabaletta 'Deh rallentate, o barbari'* ('Release me from these cruel bonds') [24] is another example of Verdi's genius for making a theatrically vivid *précis* of the complexity of the 'real' dramatic situation. Initially Azucena and Luna are simply pitted against one another. In Azucena's verse Verdi decided that there was simply no time for the contrasts of mood implicit in Cammarano's lines. The pitiful entreaty suggested by the opening is simply ignored, swept up into the prevailing passion of vehement denunciation. The double-dotted rhythm:

$$\text{♩\hspace{-0.3em}.\hspace{-0.2em}.♪ \quad ♩\hspace{-0.3em}.\hspace{-0.2em}.♪}$$

is the chief means of expressing this vehemence: first applied to a reiterated monotone A; then to vaulting and plunging leaps; finally *declamato ppp*, to mysterious chromatic seventh progressions. Luna's retort, apparently much slighter — it has only two phrases — in fact achieves equal weight by virtue of its thrilling 7-bar phrases, and the menacing chromatic line added by Ferrando and the chorus. Like Azucena, he begins with obsessively reiterated As; but there are no nervous twitches here: Luna's melody is intoned with the same kind of remorseless inexorability we heard from him in the finale of Part Two. The repeat of the *cabaletta* is drastically compressed: Azucena's verse is retained in full, but instead of Luna's retort being held back as an answer, he (and the chorus) are counterpointed against it. So the vividness achieved in the first *cabaletta* statement is not weakened by mere repetition: indeed it is heightened, while at the same time the formal proprieties of the *cabaletta* are observed.

Elizabeth Connell as Azucena at ENO (photo: Mike Humphrey)

No. 11 Scene and Aria

Manrico is the last of the principals to be given his solo scene and aria; he is depicted as lover and as hero. But so far has the action progressed, that there is no question, as there might have been in Part One, of his representing these qualities in any ideal, abstract way: both are conditioned by the sombre and ominous circumstances. In 'Ah si, ben mio' ('When Holy Church') [26] the *cantabile*, he addresses Leonora not as an ardent young wooer, but as a protector, even as a spiritual guide, and it is the function of the preceding recitative to show Leonora's urgent need for such a lover. Her fragility, her sense of impending doom, are the motives that Verdi chooses to emphasize by the sombre agitation of the prelude, and by breaking into the generally neutral declamation with a searing phrase of *arioso* propelled on a funeral march rhythm: 'Di qual tetra luce il nostro imen risplende' ('What unhappy shadows have come to cloud our marriage').

Although Manrico has not yet led Leonora to the altar the tone of 'Ah si, ben mio' is rather one of valediction than of ardent anticipation; and it concludes with a vision of death in battle as a means of entering earlier into that paradise where they will be united forever. This idea — of rising above the present by the sublimation of passion — prompts the most remarkable example in the whole opera of a slowly evolving aria, unfolding in full splendour only as it reaches the final phrases. Not only are the words reflected in melodies of ever-growing fervour, not only does the *tessitura* mount steadily into ever more exalted regions, but the key scheme too progresses from the ill-omens of the present (F minor), through the possible destiny of death on the battle-field (A b minor), to close in radiant serenity (D b major).

The greater part of the following *allegro* is given over to Ruiz's message and Manrico's first reaction to it. Initially the irony is sharpened by a brief episode, sketching the interrupted wedding ceremony. It is a remarkable inspiration, combining, in the contrapuntal antiphony of the voices, a note of rapture with a suggestion both of haste and precariousness. This feverish quality is heightened by the solemnity given to the supporting chords by the organ.

The *cabaletta* 'Di quella pira' ('That fierce inferno') may seem technically a little simplistic — do not the flickering semiquavers of the 'pira' monopolize its rhythmic flow unduly? – and psychologically a little crass — does not Leonora deserve something better than the perfunctory minor-key episode addressed to her? But as a release of the sombre tensions built up in the early part of the scene it is infallibly effective. The peculiarly obsessive themes in the Azucena/Luna duet here find a companion piece, similarly urgent and inexorable, but this time coloured by the trumpeting splendour of the heroic tenor voice.

Part Four: The Execution

The fourth act is centred around Leonora and her attempt to rescue Manrico from the clutches of Luna. For Manrico's mission at the end of Part Three has failed: he and Azucena are now imprisoned in Luna's castle and the rebel fortress has fallen to the royalist forces. Leonora, however, has so far eluded the count, and she has with her a phial of poison. As Luna emerges from his castle meditating on the jealousy that drives him from crime to crime, Leonora accosts him, and pleads for Manrico's life. Luna is deaf to her appeal, until she offers herself as the price for Manrico's freedom; then he assents. While Luna gives instructions to a guard, Leonora drinks the poison.

In their prison, Azucena and Manrico await death on the morrow. Azucena is tormented by the thought of sharing the same hideous fate as her mother, but Manrico comforts her and she sleeps. Leonora enters and urges Manrico

James King and Leontyne Price as Manrico and Leonora at Covent Garden in 1970 (photo: Anthony Crickmay)

to escape. Refusing to leave without her, he suspects the bargain she may have made with Luna and, as she makes no denial, denounces her as faithless. But when she sinks dying to his feet, he is overcome with remorse. At this point Luna appears: frustrated once again, he consigns Manrico immediately to the scaffold and forces the gipsy to watch the execution from the cell window. As Manrico dies, Azucena reveals his identity: her mother has been avenged!

No. 12 Scena, Aria and Miserere

With the *Miserere* scene we reach one of the supreme achievements of Italian Romantic melodrama: the situation is emotionally and scenically enthralling; from first bar to last Verdi is at the peak of his form; and as a result it provides a magnificent demonstration of the dramatic potential of the traditional structures. More vividly and poignantly than anywhere else in the opera the *scena* performs its traditional functions: making audible the smothering darkness of the scene in the murky clarinet and bassoon textures of the prelude, and disposing of the greater part of the recitative quietly and expeditiously in order to give expressive force to its key moments. Notice particularly the glorious *arioso* at the close, a pattern of slurred drooping phrases in which Leonora wafts her love to the imprisoned Manrico; the subtle alchemy of pathetic fallacy has produced this climax by transfiguring the 'sighing breezes' heard previously in the orchestra.

In *'D'amor sull'ali rosee'* ('Breeze of the night go seek him') [28], one may first admire the gradation of mood in Bardare's verses (Cammarano had

Montserrat Caballé as Leonora at Covent Garden in 1975 (photo: Anthony Crickmay)

apparently envisaged *'Quel suon, quello preci'* ('That sound and those voices') [30] as the *cantabile*) and appreciate the way in which this encourages Verdi's fondness for continuously unfolding melodies. Effortless as the melodic inspiration may seem, it does incorporate some detailed reflections of this text: it is not chance that the opening phrase is shaped to suggest something floating upwards — like the message of love being wafted to Manrico's tower; nor that when Leonora prays that Manrico may waken to dreams of love, the voice and flute sing together in parallel sixths.

Having added this aria to Cammarano's original libretto, Verdi found himself with a formidable amount of material to pack into the *tempo di mezzo*.

Filippo Sanjust's design for Act Four, scene one, at Covent Garden in 1964.

The masterly coherence of this episode — the richest and most thrilling *tempo di mezzo* in all Italian opera — is perhaps due to the fact that Verdi encourages us to experience the whole scene from Leonora's point of view. The death-knell and the funeral chant might have remained the mere apparatus of gothic horror, had not Leonora's imagination transmuted them into a shuddering of dread: 'That sound and those voices'. A rhythmic vibration, albeit *ppp*, fills the whole orchestra, just as in Leonora's mind *'cupo terror'* (gloomy terror) fills the air. And against this extraordinary evocation Leonora sings a phrase, equally shuddering in character, which reels into the cadence in a lamenting sequence of *appoggiaturas*.

From the tower is heard the voice of Manrico, once more the simple troubadour, singing his farewell to Leonora. Again Verdi makes us hear him as Leonora does: he does not fuss about the precise connotations of Cammarano's text, but provides a song that, like the troubadour's serenade in Act One, might be described as ideally, almost celestially, passionate and heroic. For the rest of the *tempo di mezzo* these elements are woven into an ever denser pattern.

'Tu vedrai che amore' ('You will see that my devotion'), the *cabaletta*, is comparatively conventional — after so magnificent a musical tableau anything would be. But apart from providing the emotional energy to drive the action forward, it is not lacking in fine points. Notice how Leonora's music has now acquired something of the insistent determination of much of the other

characters' music. But that purposefulness does not disregard the dramatic context; it is almost entirely expressed in an agitated *sotto voce*, and the overall melodic shape suggests a yearning out of present darkness for the light of love.

No. 13 Scena and Duet

Luna's ascendancy over Leonora is clinched towards the end of the *primo tempo* by a snarling unison phrase, doubled by trumpets and woodwind as well as strings. Leonora is reduced to a pitiful sighing descent to the cadence. In the *cantabile* 'Mira, di acerba lagrime' ('Witness these bitter tears') [33] the duettists take on almost tangible form. Over and over again Leonora's phrases reach up in entreaty, mounting to the final line *'calpesta il mio cadavere, ma salva il Trovator'* (trample on my corpse but save the troubadour). The pulsing of horns and middle strings depict something of Luna's emotions, but his answer acquires its expressive force primarily from its rhythm: heavily accented, grim and relentless. In the final duet stages of the movement his dominance is given musical form by a partial reprise of his verse, to which Leonora contributes no more than a sighing descant.

The *cabaletta* is the only example in the opera in which the singers are not clearly differentiated in style. The music, in a mood of breathless, almost agitated joy, is shared out between them. There is no regular repetition, simply two fragmentary reprises, separated by a new section of genuine duetting and by one telling moment of suspense, when Luna reminds Leonora of her oath.

No. 14 Last Finale

As the opera approaches its catastrophe, the ebb and flow of passion and the accelerating pace of the incidents prompt Verdi to abandon the traditional operatic forms that have so far served him so well. The finale conforms to no standard pattern but accommodates a wide range of subsidiary structures, some of them of notable freedom. After a soft and solemn prelude and some recitative, the first section of the finale can best be described as a dramatic *scena* for Azucena. As she agonizes over the prospect of the pyre on which she is to die, *'Stride la vampa'* makes a second hallucinatory return. Then as her frenzy subsides, Manrico's tender recitative soothes her into the *cantabile*, *'Si, la stanchezza'* ('Yes, let me sleep') [36]. The particular glory of this — another example of an aria beautifully matched to its dramatic context — is the way Manrico's lullaby-like refrains prompt its changes of style, from lethargic weariness in verse one to a sweet drowsy nostalgia for her distant homeland in verse two.

The next musical high point comes with the trio in which, while Azucena sleeps, Manrico accuses Leonora of infidelity, an example of Verdi's skill at reconciling the demands of the theatre with a craftsmanlike elaboration of the musical form. In Manrico's accusation not a word is lost: as in an accompanied recitative, the orchestra seconds the voice antiphonally. Then his grief is transformed into a wild, grim song, its cutting effect enhanced by the doubling on oboe, trumpet and cello, while the key-word *'infame'* is emphasized by an orchestral slither onto the dissonant B♭. To Manrico's relentless iterations, Leonora responds by runnning through the whole gamut seeking the eloquence to persuade him of her good faith. Then, when the minds of the protagonists have been indelibly depicted, Verdi steps back and lets us take in the whole tableau, including the sleeping Azucena as she dreams of her homeland. The final lyrical crisis, the reconciliation of the lovers as Leonora dies, obviously lacks the structural coherence of the earlier episodes. These various lyrical movements are linked by *tempi di mezzo* and after Leonora's death the orchestra takes over again, sweeping all the characters towards the final catastrophe in the black key of E♭ minor.

Antonio García Gutiérrez's 'El trovador'

Donald Shaw

The first night of *El trovador* (*The Troubadour*) on March 1, 1836 at the Príncipe Theatre in Madrid marked a turning point in the history of Spanish drama. Its author, Antonio García Gutiérrez (1813–1884), at twenty-three, was all but unknown, his only previous stage productions having been translations. In 1833 he had run away from home in southern Spain to be a writer, but in despair at his apparent failure he impulsively joined the army instead, Spain being in the middle of a Civil War. Thus at the end of the first performance he had to borrow a presentable coat to put over his uniform in order to take a curtain-call. It was the first time a playwright had ever been called on to the stage by the public in a Spanish theatre.

This young soldier from the provinces in three short years in the capital had made up all the ground which had been broken by his elders in the Spanish romantic movement, without having shared the contact which some of them had had in exile with the theatre outside Spain. The romantics, breaking with stiff imitations of French neo-classical tragedies, had returned to the old tradition of Spanish theatre created by Lope de Vega (1562–1635) in which plot was paramount, the tone was popular and tragi-comic and the subjects often harked back to famous incidents in Spanish history or legend. The Duke of Rivas, Larra and others revived the vogue for historical and pseudo-historical plays with their appeal to nationalistic feelings, their colourful settings and striking episodes. But the outlook of the romantic dramatists was very different from that of Lope and his successors. Comic scenes and characters largely disappear; happy endings are usually eliminated; the hero and heroine, who acknowledge love as the only absolute, are doomed to struggle unavailingly against forces which gradually shatter their illusion and destroy their lives. The prime example is Juan Eugenio Hartzenbusch's *Los amantes de Teruel* (*The Lovers of Teruel*, 1837), based on an old legend, in which the Lovers, deprived of all hope of love-fulfilment, die as simply and inevitably as a watch stops when its mainspring breaks. We do not know where García Gutiérrez found the inspiration for his play, outside his own imagination. Its historical period, the Wars of Aragon 1410–1412, when the kingdom was left without a ruler, is recognisable enough, but the rest appears to be pure fiction. What is certain is that the young dramatist had recognized the possibilities of the new movement, analysed its manner and techniques and put them together in a play which caught the crest of the wave. He became famous overnight. The play ran for a fortnight (a huge success in those days), was revived twice in the same year and was soon being played all over Spain. The leading critics of the time saw it as setting the seal on the triumph of romanticism on the Spanish stage.

It is hard at first sight to see why. The play today, though often re-printed, is hardly ever performed and is remembered outside Spain chiefly as the original of *Il Trovatore*. Nor did García Gutiérrez ever again score a success like it, even with *Simón Bocanegra* (1843) from which Verdi also took a libretto. The explanation of this failure does not lie only in the cruelly short runs of Spanish plays in the 19th century, which drove other romantics besides García Gutiérrez to hasty improvisation. It lies in the ambivalent outlook of the romantic writers themselves. Many of them had suffered long periods of exile under the reactionary Ferdinand VII, whose reign lasted from 1814 to 1833. They had become aware that the old world-view was in crisis. The 'European Crisis of Conscience' had been provoked by (among many other factors) the attacks of writers such as Voltaire on the traditional religious and providentialist view of life, by the collapse of 18th-century optimistic rationalism before the impact of critical thinkers like Hume and Kant, and by the immense social and ideological upheavals consequent on the spread of French revolutionary doctrines and the outbreak of the Napoleonic Wars. From the closing years of the 18th-century, the belief, among younger writers and intellectuals, even in Spain, in a fatherly world made according to God-ordained design, began to give way sporadically to our more modern and more tragic sense of life. Not for nothing was the greatest Spanish romantic poem, written between 1840 and 1842 by José de Espronceda, called *El diablo mundo* (*The Devil World*). Man's ability to make sense of the human condition either through faith or with the light of reason no longer seemed obvious. The greatest (and the only really surviving) Spanish romantic plays, Mariano José de Larra's *Macías* (1834), The Duke of Rivas's *Don Alvaro* (1835), *El trovador* itself and Hartzenbusch's *Los amantes de Teruel*, with a small handful of others, express more or less clearly a response to this crisis. Herein lies their authentic contribution to European romanticism. But the phase was short-lived. In the Spain of the 19th century the use of themes derived from the new awareness provoked misunderstanding in the audiences and fierce hostility from traditionalist critics. The romantic writers, isolated, under attack and in most cases alarmed by the implications of their own insight, began to defect. As the crest of the romantic wave passed and was followed by a trough, the more timid of them, of whom García Gutiérrez was one, swung over to a more acceptable but more superficial kind of romanticism much influenced by Sir Walter Scott. In the theatre this meant historical plays exalting the mediaeval and Golden Age traditions of honour and famous deeds of love and valour of a bygone Spain, such as José Zorrilla's *El zapatero y el rey* (*The King and the Shoemaker*, 1840) or Gertrudis Gómez de la Avellaneda's *El Príncipe de Viana* (*The Prince of Viana*, 1844), in which audiences could find relief from the political chaos and the religious strife of the country in their own time. In this way the deeper implications of the best romantic plays, which raised them above mere story-telling and pandering to national prejudices to achieve a wider human relevance, were sacrificed. García Gutiérrez's later theatre clearly exemplifies this process. That is why *El trovador*, his first and most audacious original play, is the exception on which his fame rests.

The major Spanish romantic plays, which used until the 1940s to be regarded rather patronisingly as historical extravaganzas written in imitation of 17th-century verse-drama and chiefly important as revealing the vitality of the Golden Age tradition, tend nowadays to be interpreted as symbolic rather than simply historical plays. Increasingly we are coming to see that they reveal the same preoccupations that can be seen in much of the best romantic poetry, especially of Espronceda, where equally subversive and pessimistic attitudes are expressed by cognate symbols, such as the cooling down of the sun (the failure of all that we regard as eternal and enduring), the death of an innocent child (God's injustice) or the recurrent prison-symbol (of man trapped in an oppresive existence with only death as the outlet). Undoubtedly, however, the romantics longed to conquer the stage, both because after the tumultuous reception in Paris of Victor Hugo's *Hernani* in 1830 it seemed the ordained battle-ground of the movement, and because printed texts of successful or notorious plays sold in large numbers and could be expected to be more influential than tiny editions of books of poetry or little magazines. Novels were not at this time an influential genre in Spain.

The basic theme of the plays we are here concerned with is love, crossed by adverse fate, leading to death. Love, that is, has been elevated to the status of the main support of human existence, while fate's hostility implies a world where comforting belief in a benevolent Providence watching over man has been lost. Concretely this formula is expressed in terms of dramatic conflicts in which the love-ideal is incarnated in the hero and heroine, while malignant fate hovers behind their adversaries. In the most famous example, Rivas's *Don Alvaro*, on which Verdi based *La forza del destino* (*The Force of Destiny*), the conflict is rendered more explicit by causing both the lovers to embrace the religious life. In this way, when fate breaks in, religion is shown to be powerless against it.

Garcia Gutiérrez's *El trovador* contains a similar conflict. Once more, when love's fulfilment seems impossible, Leonor takes refuge in a convent. Despite an attempt by the Count of Luna's men-at-arms to prevent it, she actually professes and takes the veil. This is the dominating feature of the centre of Garcia Gutiérrez's play. Its consequences are of fundamental importance. For when, in his turn, Manrique forces an entry into the convent in order to persuade Leonor to flee from it with him, he finds her, in the crucial scene, already dressed in the habit of her order, praying before a crucifix in her cell. Although she is remorseful that her recent vows have not sufficed to drive the memory of him from her mind, she has taken the irrevocable step. None the less, when he appears, she has little hesitation in deserting the religious life to join him. Human love triumphs explicitly over love of God. Thus it is with crushing irony that Manrique is forced by fate in the next act to reward her sacrifice by deserting her in order to save Azucena whom he believes to be his mother. When at the end of the play Leonor resorts to suicide as part of her plan to save Manrique, she adds to her account a further mortal sin.

This dimension of *El trovador* is of basic relevance to its structure. It has five acts, in contrast to the four of the libretto. Cammarano has condensed Acts Two and Three of the original into a single act, and from the standpoint of the story-line this is perfectly logical. An essential feature of Garcia Gutiérrez's play is, however, sacrificed. The latter deliberately arranged the design of his plot so that, at the end of Act Two, Manrique arrives at the convent in time to prevent Leonor from taking her vows. But fate, in the shape of the Count's men, intervenes precisely at that moment to stop Manrique from abducting her or persuading her not to become a nun. The chance is lost; the lovers are separated in the critical instant. So that when Manrique finally makes his appeal to Leonor in Act Three it is in a sense too late. To underline the irony, Azucena's quasi-revelation to Manrique of his true parentage takes place between his first visit to the convent and his second, more successful one.

It is quite clear that Garcia Gutiérrez was fully aware of what he was doing. His whole object in postponing Leonor's decision until after she has made her vows is to emphasise on the one hand the role of fate and on the other the victory of human love. Lorca, an avid reader of romantic plays, may well have remembered this famous precedent when he in turn postponed the lovers' elopement in *Blood Wedding* until after the ceremony. Cammarano was obliged to run together Manrique's two visits to the convent, and to prevent Leonor from making her vows, partly no doubt for reasons of brevity, but also, surely, because *Il Trovatore* was to be staged for the first time in the Papal States under vigilant censorship. Verdi himself had wished Leonora to be carried off by Manrico after making her vows, as in the original, but was overruled. Without disrespect to Cammarano, who was a first class librettist, it must be said that the restrictions under which he was working compelled him to shorten and alter García Gutiérrez's play in such a way that some of its meaning is obscured. We are still left, however, with a superbly dramatic plot.

It has three stages or tiers, each rising to a striking climax before leading on to the next. The first conflict between the Count and Manrique produces a splendid curtain-scene as the two leave with drawn swords to fight their duel. As in *Il Trovatore* itself, the real defect of Act One is the opening, where García Gutiérrez seems to have been at a loss for a device to disguise his exposition and fell back on bare narration. But thereafter the first act of the Spanish original is faultless. Leonor is forced by her brother (a character dispensed with by Cammarano) to choose between marrying the Count or entering a convent, a scene which effectively enlists the audience's sympathies on her behalf. Her lyrical lament offers a fine contrast to Manrique's unexpected and virile entrance, burning as he is with jealousy of his rival. The tone moves dramatically from the minor to the major key. As the lovers make it up, the Count appears and the act ends on a note of proud defiance and suspense as the two men go out to fight.

Acts Two and Three contain, as we have seen, the symbolic crux of García Gutiérrez's play. Equally they contain the rising plane of the action, culminating in Leonor's decision to forsake her vows and join her lover. Fate, however, intervenes afresh in Act Four when Azucena is captured. The event confirms Leonor's apprehensions that she will be punished for breaking her vows, and fulfils a premonitory dream of Manrique's. Torn between love for her and love for the gipsy he still believes to be his mother, Manrique decides to risk all in a bid to save her. The lovers' brief interval of happiness is over. The last act of *El trovador* is masterly. Time and again throughout García Gutiérrez's play we find extremely effective juxtapositions of scenes of lyricism or sinister quiet with others of high drama and action. Here at the end this technique reaches a climax. García Gutiérrez introduced two, short, deliberately low-key pause-scenes to separate Leonor's passionate lamentations at the opening from her sudden reappearance in the middle to beg for Manrique's release. Similarly, the slow, emotional scene between Manrique and Azucena in the dungeon contrasts admirably with the grandiose finale.

What Verdi seems to have seen in *El trovador* was a work which offered a libretto of remarkable power and originality. He wrote to Cammarano of its 'fine theatrical effects' and of its being 'above all something original and out of the ordinary'. What Cammarano seems to have seen was something a little more conventional: a play which could be cut down to four short acts, each of which had its own dramatic conflict and each of which rose to a splendid climax. Four successive springs of tension lead to four gripping curtain-scenes. Stripped of some of its symbolic elements the play is all excitement. And the characters are made to match. None of them is really reflective. It is not by chance, for example, that Manrique, unlike his great counterpart in Spanish romantic drama, Rivas's *don Alvaro*, has no soliloquies. He is, like Hugo's *Hernani*, '*une force qui va*'. On his first entry in Act One he is already at a white heat of passion. When in the convent he finds Leonor already a bride of Christ in remorseful prayer, he shows no signs of understanding or sympathising with her situation, but instead peremptorily demands that she should break her vows and flee with him. When his supposed mother is captured, he has no other thought but to risk all, Leonor's love included, to save her. Manrique, that is, shows from the outset all that characteristic rapidity of emotional reaction which we associate with the more extreme romantic heroes. The appearance of such heroes on the serious stage reminds us that the romantics were in revolt against rational as well as social restraints.

They found in dramas set in the turbulent past opportunities to build into their plays the kind of extreme situations which gave scope for the expression of elemental passions. For Verdi — who revelled in strong situations — a figure like Manrique, whose personality and circumstances impel him from one to another of them, was clearly inspiring. In fact, much of the melodrama and extravagance of plot which we associate with Italian grand opera derives directly from the determination of the romantics, whose plays supplied so many librettos, to break completely out of neo-classical and rationalistic ideas of decorum. When the movement had run its course and gone out of fashion, romantic play-situations were only too easy to parody. This is not surprising when we think of Azucena's story in *Il Trovatore*; confusion over babies was an obvious ploy for Oscar Wilde in *The Importance of Being Ernest* and a recurrent Gilbert-and-Sullivan theme.

In *El trovador* Leonor tends to outshine Manrique. It is she, not he, who strikes the true romantic attitudes. She has the soliloquies. She expresses the struggle between human love and love of God as the groundwork of existence. In addition there is the ironic symmetry of Acts Three and Four. Her choice between her salvation in Heaven and her happiness on earth is rewarded by Manrique's being faced with the choice between love of her and the obligation to try to save Azucena. This symmetry of choice and Leonor's heroic stratagem in Act Five to save her lover emphasise Leonor's stature in the Spanish original. Inevitably, once Cammarano collapses Act Three into Act Two, the symmetry is destroyed and part of Leonor's stature is lost. In addition, one of the more important scenes in *El trovador* is that in which Manrique confesses to the aristocratic Leonor that he is the son of a mere gipsy. To the romantics, figures on the margin of society — the gipsy, the beggar, the criminal, the prostitute, the clown — had a special significance, often as symbols of freedom or revolt. Leonor reveals her romantic outlook as well as the depth of her love for Manrique by accepting him despite his origins, or perhaps because of them. Similarly she never for an instant shows the slightest interest in inducing Manrique to marry her. Indeed, how could she, bound as she was by her prior vows? Instead she proudly refers to him as her lover. In Cammarano's libretto, however, she is rather more conventionalised in Act Three. The scene in which Manrique reveals his origin to her derives its whole effect precisely from the fact that they are about to marry (there being no impediment in this case) when Azucena's capture is announced. Thus in the opera Leonora only reveals her character fully in the last act.

Azucena's role in the play, as Verdi clearly saw, is much more significant than that of a picturesque character around whom he could build a series of colourful musical tableaux such as the 'anvil' chorus. She is in fact the reverse of the conventional wheedling fortune-teller or unscrupulous go-between. He perceived 'the novelty and strangeness of her character' and 'her two great passions', that is to say her demonic desire to avenge her mother and her quasi-maternal love for Manrique (who has supplanted her dead child). Unlike Rigoletto, whose vengeance stems from the outrage to his daughter, Azucena can only carry out her revenge at the expense of her substitute son's life. It is through Azucena's terrible silence at critical moments that fate operates to destroy the love-ideal. Without her presence, only social rank would have separated Manrique from Leonor, and this could have been overcome by his prowess in battle. Her dead child stands between the lovers just as old Calatrava, killed unintentionally by don Alvaro, stands between hero and heroine in Rivas's play. With Azucena in the background, the lovers' idyll is constantly threatened. When she is captured, they are doomed.

The original version of the play contained a mixture of prose and verse, as was common at the time. It is rather extraordinary, however, that although Azucena is in one sense the mainspring of the action and continuously provides a marvellously sinister contrast to the idealised passion of the lovers, her story in Act Three should be told in cold prose. In the opera, this frankly incredible incident benefits in the telling from the audience's more ready suspension of disbelief and from the fact that it comes across in verse and music. Almost as strange is the fact that one of the last, moving, scenes between Azucena and Manrique in the dungeon near the end is also in prose. Garcia Gutiérrez eventually versified the whole play. This second version appeared in 1851, by which time eight editions of the work as originally performed, including one in 1851 as well, had appeared. It is therefore far more likely that Verdi and Cammarano used the original version, though we cannot be sure.

Garcia Gutiérrez's verse is fluid and melodious but rather bare of imagery. He used standard combinations of eight-syllable lines, except in major scenes between the lovers which move up into an eleven-syllable 'heroic' form. A good example of the former is Azucena's short song in Act Three describing her mother's death at the stake:

Bramando está el pueblo indómito,	Uncontrolled the mob are roaring,
de la hoguera en derredor;	round the burning funeral pyre
al ver ya cerca la víctima	as they see the victim approaching
gritos lanza de furor.	they howl aloud with fury.
Allí viene; el rostro pálido,	She comes; her face is ashen,
sus miradas de terror,	her eyes, bright with terror,
brillan de la llama trémula	shine in the sinister glare
al siniestro resplendor.	of the flickering flames.

Less dramatic is the end of Leonor's main soliloquy:

Mi juventud	My youth
los tiranos marchitaron,	was by tyrranous enemies withered
y a mi vida prepararon	and for my life's end was prepared
junto al altar el ataúd.	a coffin beside the altar.
Illusiones engañosas,	Deceitful illusions,
livianas como el placer,	impalpable as pleasure itself,
no aumentéis mi padecer . . .	do not increase my torment . . .
¡Sois por mi mal tan hermosas!	You are, to my sorrow, so lovely!

We can contrast the rhetorical resonances of the heroic form as Manrique reproaches Leonor for hesitating to break her vows:

¡Esto aguardaba yo! Cuando creía	Was it for this I waited! When I believed
que más que nunca enamorada y tierna	that more tenderly loving than before
me esperabas ansiosa, así te encuentro,	you anxiously awaited my coming, I find you thus
¡sorda a mi ruego, a mis halagos fría!	deaf to my pleas, cold to my caresses!
¿Y tiemblas, di, de abandonar las aras	Say then: do you fear to abandon the altars
donde tu puro afecto y tu hermosura sacrificaste a Dios?	on which your purest love and beauty you sacrificed to God?

To conclude: in *El trovador* Verdi and Cammarano found a play which could be condensed into four fast-moving acts in which the interludes of lyrical outpouring never really interfere with the suspense. Firm outlines of character in the protagonists are matched by a variety of colourful settings. Above all the fact that the original play was so completely *theatrical* played straight into the librettist's hands. Once some of its symbolic and morally subversive elements had been discarded, Verdi was left with a well-articulated plot rising through successive episodes of conflict to a memorable finale in which tension survives right up to Azucena's last triumphant words.

Thematic Guide

Many of the themes from the opera have been identified in the articles by numbers in square brackets, which refer to the themes set out on these pages. The themes are also identified by the numbers in brackets at the corresponding points in the libretto, so that the words can be related to the musical themes.

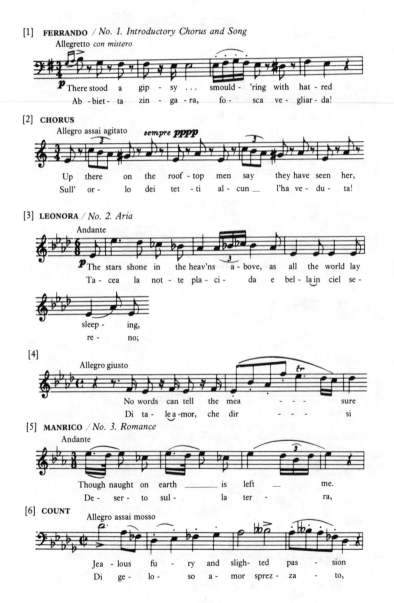

[1] **FERRANDO** / *No. 1. Introductory Chorus and Song*

Allegretto *con mistero*

p There stood a gip - sy ... smould - 'ring with hat - red
Ab - biet - ta zin - ga - ra, fo - sca ve - gliar - da!

[2] **CHORUS**

Allegro assai agitato *sempre pppp*

Up there on the roof - top men say they have seen her,
Sull' or - lo dei tet - ti al - cun _ l'ha ve - du - ta!

[3] **LEONORA** / *No. 2. Aria*

Andante

p The stars shone in the heav'ns a - bove, as all the world lay
Ta - cea la not - te pla - ci - da e bel - la in ciel se -

sleep - ing,
re - no;

[4]

Allegro giusto

No words can tell the mea - - - sure
Di ta - le a - mor, che dir - - - si

[5] **MANRICO** / *No. 3. Romance*

Andante

Though naught on earth _ is left _ me.
De - ser - to sul - la ter - ra,

[6] **COUNT**

Allegro assai mosso

Jea - lous fu - ry and sligh- ted pas - sion
Di ge - lo - so a - mor sprez - za - to,

35

[7] LEONORA, MANRICO

Allegro assai mosso

L. Stay a mo - ment and hear my en - trea - ty
  Un i -stan - te al - men di - a lo - co,

M. All his boast - ing is vain __ and use - less
   Del su - per - bo è va - na l'i - ra;

[8] CHORUS OF GIPSIES / *No. 4.*

Allegro
cresc.
pp

See how the sha - dow - y clouds are fly - ing, day is re -
Ve - di! le fo - sche not - tur - ne__ spo - glie__ de' cie - li

turn - ing to light the ____ hea - vens.
sve - ste l'im - men - sa ____ vol - ta;

[9]

Allegro
f

Who cheers the days __ of the poor __ rov - ing gip - sy?
Chi del gi - ta - no i gior - ni ab - bel - la?

[10] AZUCENA / *Canzone*

Allegretto

Fierce flames are rag ____ ing see ____ how the
Stri - de la vam - pa! la ____ fol - la in-

noi ____ sy crowd
do - - mi - ta

[11] AZUCENA / *No. 5. Narrative*

Andante mosso
p

They brought her, fet - ter'd and pow'r - less
Con - dot - ta el - l'e - ra in cep - pi

[12] MANRICO / *from No. 6. Duet*

Allegro

As we - strug - gled he stum - bled be - fore me
Mal reg - gen - do al - l'a - spro as - sal - to,

[13] AZUCENA

Allegro sostenuto

Yet no an - gel voice from hea - ven shows con - cern for your sur - vi - val
Ma nell' al - ma dell' in - gra - to non par - lo del ciel un det - to,

36

[14] **AZUCENA**

Velocissimo *agitato assai*

You are still too weak to ven - - ture

Pe - ri - gliar - ti an - cor lan - guen - - te,

[15] **MANRICO**

Velocissimo

If I stay a mo - ment long - - er

Un mo - men - to puo in - vo - lar - - mi

[16] **COUNT** / *No. 7.*

Largo *cantabile*

All the stars that shine a - bove me

Il ba - len del suo sor - ri - so

[17] **CHORUS**

Allegro assai mosso *sotto voce*

The hour, the hour, has come, has come, no more de - lay

Ar - dir, ar - dir, an - diam, an - diam, ce - lia - mo - ci

[18] **COUNT**

Allegro mosso

My hour of joy ap - roach - - es

Per me o - ra fa - ta - - le,

[19] **NUNS** / *No. 8. Finale*

Andante

Here in this world of sor - row, daugh - ter of Eve re - mem - ber

Ah! se l'er - ror t'in - gom - bra, o fi - glia d'E - va, i - ra - i,

[20] **LEONORA**

Andante mosso *con tutta forza di sentimento*

Oh can it be, can I be - lieve

E deg - gio e pos - so cre - der - lo?

[21] **SOLDIERS** / *No. 9. Chorus*

Allegro

Though to - day we take our lei - sure dawn will

Or co' da - di, ma fra po - co gio - che -

bring a stern - er plea - sure

rem ben al - tro gio - co!

Allegro moderato maestoso *grandioso*

Let all the trum - pets set e - choes re - ply - ing when they
Squil - li,e - cheg - gi la trom - ba guer - rie - ra, chia - mi all'

sum - mon us to bat - tle and to plun - - der.
ar - mi,al - la pu - gna,all' as - sal - - to,

[23] **AZUCENA** / *No. 10 Trio*

Andante mosso

Though my life was poor and low - ly
Gior - ni po - ve - ri vi - ve - a,

[24] **AZUCENA**

Allegro

Re - lease me from these cru - el bonds, have mer - cy I im - plore you
Deh! ral - len - ta - te,o bar ba - ri, le a - cer - be mie ri - tor - te

[25] **COUNT**

Allegro

p

The trea - cher - ous Man - ri - co is your son, you cra - zy gip - sy
Tua pro - le,o tur - pe zin - ga - ra, co - lui, quel tra - di - to - re?

[26] **MANRICO**

Adagio *cantabile con espressione*

When ho - ly church has blessed our love our hearts will grieve no long - er
Ah, si, ben mio; coll' es - se - re io tuo, tu mia con - sor - te,

[27] **MANRICO**

Allegro

That fierce in - fer - - no her cru - el sen - - tence
Di quel - la pi - ra l'or - ren - do fo - - co

[28] **LEONORA** / *No. 12. Aria*

Adagio *con espressione*

tr

Breeze of the night ... go seek _____ him
D'a - mor sull' a - - li ro - se - e

[29] CHORUS

Andante assai sostenuto *a mezza voce*

Lord have mer - cy up - on a soul de - part - ing
Mi - se - re - re d'un' al - ma già vi - ci - na

[30] LEONORA

Andante assai sostenuto

That sound and those voi - ces
Quel suon, quel - le pre - ci

[31] MANRICO

Andante assai sostenuto

Ah! _____ when will death con - sole _____ me
Ah! _____ che la mor - te o - gno - ra

[32] LEONORA

Andante assai sostenuto

Could I _____ could I _____ for - get you?
Di te, _____ di - te _____ scor - dar - mi!

[33] LEONORA / No. 13. Duet

Andante con moto

Wit - ness these bit - ter tears of mine see all the grief I suf - fer
Mi - ra, dia - cer - be la - gri - me spar - go al tuo pie - de un ri - o!

[34] COUNT

Andante con moto

Ah! could he die a thou-sand deaths, I'd ne - ver be con - ten - ted
Ah! dell' in - de - gno ren - de - re vor - rei peg - gior la sor - te,

[35] LEONORA

Allegro brillante *molto vivace*

He lives! I can - not speak for joy, to thank you oh Heav-'nly Fa - ther
Vi - vrà! Con - ten - de il giu - bi - lo i det - ti a me, Si - gno - re,

[36] AZUCENA / No. 14. Finale

Andantino *a mezza voce*

Yes, let me sleep for my limbs are wear - y
Sì, la stan - chez - za m'op - pri - me, o fi - glio,

39

[37] MANRICO

Andantino *a mezza voce*

Rest now dear mo - ther ... calm all your ter - rors
Ri - po - sa, o ma - dre, Id - di - o con - ce - da

[38] AZUCENA

Andantino

Safe in our moun - tains
Ai no - stri mon - ti

[39] MANRICO

Andante

So ____ you have sold ___ your - self to that ty - rant
Ha ____ quest' in - fa - me l'a - mor ___ ven - du - to!

[40] LEONORA

Andante

your an - ger blinds you and makes you, and makes - you heart - less
O co - me l'i - ra ti ren - de, ti ren - de ___ cie - co!

[41] LEONORA

Andante

Ra - ther than live to be his bride ___ I die for you my love
Pri - ma che d'al - tri vi - ve - re ___ i - o vol - li tua mo - rir!

Design for Act Three by Filippo Sanjust for Visconti's Covent Garden production in 1964.

Il Trovatore

Opera in four parts by Giuseppe Verdi

Libretto by Salvatore Cammarano
with additions by Leone Emmanuele Bardare
after the play *El trovador* by Antonio García Gutiérrez

English translation by Tom Hammond

Il Trovatore was first performed at the Teatro Apollo, Rome on January 19, 1853. The first performance in England was at Covent Garden on May 10, 1855. It was first performed in New York on May 2, 1855.

The numbers in square brackets refer to the Thematic Guide.

Katherine Pring as Azucena at ENO (photo: John Garner)

CHARACTERS

The Count of Luna *a young noble in the service of*   *baritone*
      the Prince of Aragon

Leonora *a lady-in-waiting to the Princess of Aragon*   *soprano*

Azucena *an old gipsy woman*   *mezzo-soprano*

Manrico *an officer in the army of Prince Urgel, and*   *tenor*
      supposed son of Azucena

Ferrando *officer in the Count of Luna's army*   *bass*

Inez (Ines) *Leonora's attendant and confidante*   *soprano*

Ruiz *Manrico's henchman*   *tenor*

An old gipsy   *bass*

A messenger   *tenor*

Companions of Leonora and Nuns, Retainers of the Count, Soldiers, Gipsies

The action takes place partly in Biscay and partly in **Aragon**.

Epoch: the beginning of the fifteenth century.

Marietta Alboni as Azucena in Paris (Raymond Mander and Joe Mitchenson Theatre Collection)

Part One: The Duel

Scene One. *A vestibule in the Aliaferia Palace. On one side, a door leading to the Count di Luna's apartments. Ferrando and several members of the Count's retinue are reclining by the door; a few Men-at-arms pace up and down in the background.* / *No. 1. Introductory Chorus and Song*

FERRANDO
(to the Retainers, who are almost falling asleep)

Wake up there, wake up there! Remember.	All'erta, all'erta! Il Conte
The Count himself may find you sleeping; you know him	N'è d'uopo attender vigilando; ed egli
Too well. Sometimes he watches	Talor presso i veroni
All through the night hours, beneath	Della sua cara, intere
His Leonora's window!	Passa le notti.

RETAINERS

We have seen how this jealous	Gelosia le fiere
Passion has driven him to madness!	Serpi gli avventa in petto!

FERRANDO

This Troubadour who sings at nightfall, there	Nel Trovator, che dai giardini move
In the palace gardens, is the rival he fears	Notturno il canto, d'un rivale a dritto
And curses!	Ei teme.

RETAINERS

Then in case	Dalle gravi
We grow weary and close our eyes in sleep,	Palpebre il sonno a discacciar, la vera
Will you not tell us the story of Garzia, our master's	Storia ci narra di Garzia, germano
Younger brother?	Al nostro Conte.

FERRANDO

Very well, come,	La dirò: venite
Gather close around.	Intorno a me.

(The Retainers do so.)

MEN-AT-ARMS
(also coming close)

Begin now.	Noi pure ...

RETAINERS

We're listening.	Udite, udite.

(All gather round Ferrando.)

FERRANDO

Heaven had given my old master two fine children	Di due figli vivea padre beato
Who became all his pride and joy;	Il buon Conte di Luna:
They had a nurse who watched from night till morning	Fida nutrice del secondo nato
By the side of the younger boy.	Dormia presso la cuna.
One day, just as the stars above were fading,	Sul romper dell'aurora un bel mattino
She felt danger was near;	Ella dischiude i rai;
And she saw by the child as it lay sleeping ...	E chi trova d'accanto a quel bambino?

RETAINERS, MEN-AT-ARMS

Who? Come tell us, who stood there?	Chi? ... Favella ... Chi? Chi mai?

There stood a gipsy, smouldering with hatred,	[1] Abbietta zingara, fosca vegliarda!
Symbols of sorcery circling her forehead,	Cingeva i simboli di maliarda!
Staring with evil eyes upon that infant,	E sul fanciullo, con viso arcigno,
Moaning and mumbling some foul enchantment.	L'occhio affiggea torvo, sanguigno!
Trembling with terror, the old nurse screamed and shouted . . .	D'orror compresa è la nutrice . . .
Her calls for succour re-echoed in the distance;	Acuto un grido all'aura scioglie;
In less time than I take to tell you about it,	Ed ecco, in meno che il labbro il dice,
Her yelling brought all the sleepy guards to her assistance.	I servi accorrono in quelle soglie;
They gave no quarter to the old gipsy,	E fra minacce, urli e percosse
But chased her from the palace gates without delay.	La rea discacciano ch'entrarvi osò.

RETAINERS, MEN-AT-ARMS

The evil woman was rightly punished,	Giusto quei petti sdegno commosse;
And for that outrage they made her pay.	L'infame vecchia lo provocò.

FERRANDO

She declared she had come to tell the fortune	Asserì che tirar del fanciullino
Of the infant Garzia!	L'oroscopo volea . . .
The liar! Day by day the boy grew weaker,	Bugiarda! Lenta febbre del meschino
Torn and wasted by fever.	La salute struggea!
His face was thin and pale, shivering and groaning,	Coverto di pallor, languido, affranto
All the night he lay suffering,	Ei tremava la sera,
By day he shuddered and never stopped his moaning . . .	Il dì traeva in lamentevol pianto . . .
She'd cast a spell upon him!	Ammaliato egli era!

(The Chorus shudders.)

We found that sorceress, caught her and bound her,	La fattucchiera perseguitata
That night the fierce flames flared up around her.	Fu presa, e al rogo fu condannata;
Yet though the gipsy died, she left a daughter,	Ma rimanea la maledetta
Seething with vengeance for her vile slaughter,	Figlia, ministra di ria vendetta! . . .
And in her madness she soon avenged her.	Compi quest'empia nefando eccesso! . . .
One day soon after, Garzia vanished,	Sparve il fanciullo . . . e si rinvenne
Then we discovered some smouldering embers	Mal spenta brage nel sito istesso
Just where the old gipsy herself had perished!	Ov'arsa un giorno la strega venne! . . .
Deep in the ashes we them uncovered	E d'un bambino . . . ahimè! . . . l'ossame
The smouldering skeleton of some poor child.	Bruciato a mezzo, fumante ancor!

RETAINERS, MEN-AT-ARMS

That evil gipsy and her mad daughter	Ah scellerata! . . . oh donna infame! . . .
By earth and heaven are now reviled!	Del par m'investe odio ed orror!
And the father?	E il padre?

FERRANDO

In his grief, he died soon after;	Brevi e tristi giorni vissi:
To the end he was filled with strange forebodings,	Pure ignoto del cor presentimento
Something told him the boy	Gli diceva che spento
Had not really perished. As he lay on his deathbed,	Non era il figlio; ed, a morir vicino,

44

He made our present master give him his word
That he'd seek his brother all his days ...
That was useless ...

Bramò che il signor nostro a lui giurasse
Di non cessar le indagini ... ah! fur vane! ...

MEN-AT-ARMS

What of the girl? Was she never
Seen again?

E di colei non s'ebbe
Contezza mai?

FERRANDO

She too escaped us! If I could
But find her, justice would
Be done!

Nulla contezza ... Oh, dato
Mi fosse rintracciarla
Un dì! ...

RETAINERS

But are you sure
You would know her?

Ma ravvisarla
Potresti?

FERRANDO

Twenty years
Have gone by since these happenings ...
yet I'd know her.

Calcolando
Gli anni trascorsi ... lo potrei.

MEN-AT-ARMS

If we could
Catch her, then we could send her
Down to hell, to her mother.

Sarebbe
Tempo presso la madre
All'inferno spedirla.

FERRANDO

To her mother? Men will tell you that the gipsy's
Evil spirit lingers in this palace
And hovers round us; when skies are dark and gloomy,
She comes to haunt us in strange disguises.

All'inferno? È credenza che dimori
Ancor nel mondo l'anima perduta
Dell'empia strega, e quando il cielo è nero
In varie forme altrui si mostri.

RETAINERS, SOLDIERS
(*in terror*)

We know it!

È vero!

SOLDIERS

Up there on the rooftop men say they have [2] seen her!

Sull'orlo dei tetti alcun l'ha veduta!

She comes in the shape of a bat or hyena!

In upupa o strige talora si muta!

RETAINERS

In form of a vampire she's even more evil!
At daybreak she flies away, back to the devil.

In corvo tal'altra; più spesso in civetta!
Sull'alba fuggente al par di saetta.

FERRANDO

A servant who struck her one day on the sierra
Once met her at dead of night, and died in his terror!

Morì di paura un servo del conte,
Che avea della zingara percossa la fronte!

(*They are all filled with superstitious terror.*)

She came in the shape of a bird of ill-omen;
As evening was falling he saw her approaching!
She stared at him wildly and scared him, yes, scared him,
And then she let out such a bloodthirsty yell!
At that very moment midnight sounded ...

Apparve a costui d'un gufo in sembianza,
Nell'alta quiete di tacita stanza! ...
Con occhio lucente guardava ... guardava,
Il cielo attristando d'un urlo feral!
Allor mezzanotte appunto suonava ...

(*Suddenly a bell rings out midnight in slow strokes.*)

Ah! Curses on that gipsy, that demon from hell!   Ah! sia maledetta la strega infernal!

(*The Men-at-arms run to the back; the Retainers hasten towards the door.*)

Scene Two. *The palace gardens. On the right, a marble staircase leading into the apartments. It is late at night; thick clouds cover the moon. Leonora and Inez. / No. 2. Recitative and Aria.*

INEZ

Come, wait no longer. It's long past midnight. Hurry.
The Queen has commanded
Your presence. You heard her.

Che più t'arresti? . . . L'ora è tarda: vieni.
Di te la regal donna
Chiese, l'udisti.

LEONORA

Another night will pass
And I shall not see him! . . .

Un'altra notte ancora
Senza vederlo . . .

INEZ

There is danger here,
Let me warn you! Leonora, tell me
When you first saw this knight
And came to love him.

Perigliosa fiamma
Tu nutri! . . . Oh come, dove
La primiera favilla
In te s'apprese?

LEONORA

At the tourney. He entered,
Clad in a sombre coat of mail; his shield
And helmet bore no crest or plumage,
No-one knew who he was, yet in the contest
He vanquished all rivals. There on his brow I placed
The crown of laurel. Civil war broke out soon after . . .
He disappeared . . . fled like some golden
Vision seen in my slumbers! My life seemed empty,
Day followed day . . . and then . . .

Ne'tornei. V'apparve
Bruno le vesti ed il cimier, lo scudo
Bruno e di stemma ignudo,
Sconosciuto guerrier, che dell'agone
Gli onori ottenne . . . Al vincitor sul crine
Il serto io posi . . . Civil guerra intanto
Arse . . . Nol vidi più! come l'aurato
Sogno fuggente imago! ed era volta
Lunga stagion . . . ma poi . . .

INEZ

What happened?   Che avvenne?

LEONORA

I'll tell you.   Ascolta.

The stars shone in the heavens above,
As all the world lay sleeping;
The moon high in her silver realm
Her lonely watch was keeping . . .
Then in that hour of peace and calm
Sounds of a lute came stealing,
Borne on the scented midnight air,
His secret heart revealing.
I heard a plaintive song of love,
The Troubadour was there.

[3] Tacea la notte placida
E bella in ciel sereno
La luna il viso argenteo
Mostrava lieto appieno . . .
Quando suonar per l'aere,
Infino allor si muto,
Dolci s'udiro e flebili
Gli accordi d'un liuto,
E versi melanconici
Un Trovator cantò.

In humble verses like murmured prayers
He sang of his devotion;
I listened and I heard a name
Repeated . . . it was my own! . . .
I ventured near my balcony . . .
I saw him, saw him beside me! . . .
I knew the joy that angels know,
Joy until then denied me!
His glance, his ardent vows of love
Made earth a heaven for me.

Versi di prece ed umile
Qual d'uom che prega Iddio
In quella repeteasi
Un nome . . . il nome mio! . . .
Corsi al veron sollecita . . .
Egli era! egli era desso! . . .
Gioia provai che agli angeli
Solo è provar concesso! . . .
Al core, al guardo estatico
La terra un ciel sembrò.

All that you tell me makes me quite anxious.	Quanto narrasti di turbamento
You do not know him . . . Be careful!	M'ha piena l'alma! . . . Io temo . . .

LEONORA

I love him!	Invano!

INEZ

This nameless stranger makes me suspicious.	Dubbio ma triste presentimento
He seems to waken some dark foreboding.	In me risveglia quest'uomo arcano!
Try to forget him . . .	Tenta obliarlo . . .

LEONORA

Forget him! No never!	Che dici! . . . oh basti! . . .

INEZ

Let me advise you, I am your friend.	Cedi al consiglio dell'amistà . . .
Promise!	Cedi . . .

LEONORA

To forget him? You speak an unknown	Obliarlo! Ah, tu parlasti
Language that love does not comprehend!	Detto, che intendere l'alma non sa.

No words can tell the measure	[4] Di tale amor che dirsi
Of my sincere devotion;	Mal può dalla parola,
With this new found emotion	D'amor che intendo io sola,
My heart is all on fire.	Il cor s'inebriò!
Our fates are joined for evermore;	Il mio destino compiersi
I never will forsake him.	Non può che a lui dappresso . . .
If death should come to take him,	S'io non vivrò per esso,
To die then and join him	Per esso io morirò,
Would be my one desire!	Per esso morirò!

INEZ

(May Heaven above protect her	(Non debba mai pentirsi
In all that may transpire!	Chi tanto un giorno amò!
I pray that she may never	Non debba mai pentirsi
Regret this mad desire.)	Chi tanto un giorno amò!)

(*They go up into the apartments.*)

Scene Three. *The Count. / No. 3. Recitative and Romance*

COUNT

How still the night is! By now	Tace la notte! immersa
Our most gracious Sovereign must be safely sleeping . . .	Nel sonno è, certo, la regal Signora;
But there her lady watches! O Leonora,	Ma veglia la sua dama . . . Oh! Leonora,
There by the window the glow	Tu desta sei; mel dice
Of the burning candles, lighting up the darkness,	Da quel verone, tremolante un raggio
Tells me that you're not sleeping.	Della notturna lampa . . .
Ah! . . . How this fire within me	Ah! . . . l'amorosa fiamma
Fills my soul with yearning! I'll declare my passion,	M'arde ogni fibra! . . . Ch'io ti vegga è d'uopo,
And you shall hear me . . . Courage! This is the hour	Che tu m'intenda . . . Vengo . . . A noi supremo
For which I've waited!	È tal momento . . .

(*Ardent with passion, he goes towards the stairs. Lute chords are heard; he stops.*)

The Troubadour! The madman! How dare he?	Il Trovator! Io fremo! Io fremo!

MANRICO'S VOICE
(*from the trees*)

Though naught on earth is left me,	[5] Deserto sulla terra,
Since fate of joy has bereft me,	Col rio destino in guerra,

I hope for love once more,
To cheer the Troubadour.

È sola speme un cor
Al Trovator!

COUNT

What madness! How dare he!

Oh detti! io fremo!

MANRICO'S VOICE

If I possessed that treasure
Precious beyond all measure,
Then, blest for ever more
Would be the Troubadour!

Ma s'ei quel cor possiede,
Bello di casta fede,
È d'ogni re maggior
Il Trovator!

COUNT

My rival! I cannot bear it!
She has heard him . . . comes to meet him!

Oh detti! . . . oh gelosia! . . .
Non m'inganno . . . Ella scende!

(*He wraps himself up in his cloak.*)

Scene Four. *Leonora and the Count.*

LEONORA
(*running towards the Count*)

Oh my beloved!

Anima mia!

COUNT

(What's this?)

(Che far?)

LEONORA

You come so late
Tonight to join me; my heart has been
    impatient
And counted every moment . . . But
    Heaven has guided you
Here once again to my embraces.

Più dell'usato
È tarda l'ora; io ne contai gl'istanti

Co'palpiti del core! . . . Alfin ti guida

Pietoso amor fra queste braccia . . .

MANRICO'S VOICE

Leonora!

Infida! . . .

(*The moon comes out from behind the clouds, revealing a figure with its face hidden behind a visor.*)

Scene Five. *Manrico with the above.*

LEONORA

Who are you? Ah, all these shadows here
Blinded me and deceived me.

Qual voce! . . . Ah, dalle tenebre
Tratta in errore io fui!

(*Recognizing them both, she throws herself at Manrico's feet in great agitation.*)
Those words were meant for you alone,
And not for him, believe me!
Although I was mistaken,
My vow remains unbroken . . .
To Heaven above I swear it,
My heart is yours alone!

A te credei rivolgere
L'accento, e non a lui . . .
A te, che l'alma mia
Sol chiede, sol desia . . .
Io t'amo, il giuro, t'amo
D'immenso, eterno amor!

COUNT
(*to Leonora*)

You're raving!

Ed osi?

MANRICO
(*raising Leonora*)

(Forgive, forgive me!)

(Ah, più non bramo!)

LEONORA

I love you.

Io t'amo.

MANRICO

I doubt no longer.

Ah, più non bramo!

48

COUNT

If you're a knight, proclaim yourself.	Se un vil non sei, discovriti!

COUNT

For this he shall atone!	Avvampo di furor!

LEONORA

(Oh Heaven!)	(Ohimè!)

COUNT

Come on, who are you?	Palesa il nome ...

LEONORA
(to Manrico, softly)

My love, take care! ...	Deh, per pietà! ...

MANRICO
(raising his visor)

You know me well,	Ravvisami,
Manrico's my name.	Manrico io son.

COUNT

What, you here?	Tu! ... come?
What madness! You, a rebel,	Insano temerario!
In league with Urgel! Condemned	D'Urgel seguace, a morte
As a traitor, you dare to trespass here,	Proscritto, ardisci volgerti
Inside our royal palace?	A queste regie porte?

MANRICO

Come on then! Call out your guards	Che tardi? ... or via, le guardie
This moment! Sentence your rival	Appella, ed il rivale
To face the executioner	Al ferro del carnefice
Tomorrow.	Consegna.

COUNT

Your hour of death	Il tuo fatale
Is nearer far than you may think,	Istante assai più prossimo
You madman. Follow!	È, dissennato! ... Vieni ...

LEONORA

Listen!	Conte!

COUNT

All my wrongs and injured pride	Al mio sdegno vittima
Demand that I should kill you.	È d'uopo ch'io ti sveni ...

LEONORA

Stay here, I beg you!	Oh ciel! t'arresta ...

COUNT

Follow me!	Seguimi ...

MANRICO

Lead on!	Andiam ...

LEONORA

(What shall I do?	(Che mai farò?
If I should call for help	Un sol mio grido perdere
They might arrest him ...) Listen!	Lo puote ...) M'odi ...

COUNT

No!	No!
Jealous fury and slighted passion	[6] Di geloso amor sprezzato
Fan the flames of my love and longing.	Arde in me tremendo il fuoco!
All your lifeblood, you cursed villain,	Il tuo sangue, o sciagurato,
Could not quench this fire within me!	Ad estinguerlo fia poco!

(to Leonora)

Foolish woman, you told him that you loved him!	Dirgli, o folle, 'Io t'amo' ardisti! . . .
In your love you glorify;	Ei più vivere non può . . .
Every word that you have spoken	Un accento proferisti
Has condemned this man to die!	Che a morir lo condannò!

LEONORA

Stay a moment and hear my entreaty,	[7] Un istante almen dia loco
Calm your anger! Listen to reason!	Il tuo sdegno alla ragione
I, yes, I, here alone am guilty;	Io, sol io, di tanto foco
Let me suffer for my treason!	Son, pur troppo, la cagione!
Kill me, kill me, rejoice in your vengeance,	Piombi, piombi il tuo furore
I will scorn you until I die.	Sulla rea che t'oltraggiò . . .
I'll not falter or show repentance:	Vibra il ferro in questo core,
All your power I now defy!	Che te amar non vuol, né può.

MANRICO

All his boasting is vain and useless;	[7] Del superbo è vana l'ira;
He shall pay, he'll not escape us;	Ei cadrà da me trafitto.
For the stranger whose love inspires you,	Il mortal che amor t'ispira,
By love's power shall be victorious.	Dall'amor fu reso invitto.

(to the Count)

Hopes of triumph have gone for ever . . .	La tua sorte è già compita . . .
Your last moment on earth is nigh!	L'ora omai per te suonò!
Fate has given me this woman to treasure;	Il suo core e la tua vita
By my own hand I swear you shall die!	Il destino a me serbò!

(The two rivals make off with drawn swords, and Leonora falls in a dead swoon.)

Edith Coates as Azucena at Covent Garden in 1947 (photo: Edward Mandinian)

Part Two: The Gipsy

Scene One. *A ruinous house at the foot of a mountain in Bizcaya. The back wall is almost completely broken down, and a large fire is burning there. Day is dawning. Azucena is seated by the fire. Manrico lies beside her on a mattress, wrapped up in his cloak. His helmet is at his feet and he gazes fixedly at the sword he clasps in his hands. A band of Gipsies is scattered around. / No. 4. Chorus of Gipsies.*

GIPSIES

See how the shadowy clouds are flying, [8]	Vedi! le fosche notturne spoglie
Day is returning to light the heavens;	De' cieli sveste l'immensa volta;
Night like a widow grown weary of sighing	Sembra una vedova che alfin si toglie
Throws off the garments of prayer and penance.	I bruni panni ond'era involta.
Let's start our labours! Bring us the hammers.	All'opra! All'opra! Dàgli, martella.

(They take up their blacksmith's irons. Now the men, now the women, and finally all together sing the following cantilena to the rhythmic crash of hammers on anvils.)

Who cheers the days of the poor roving gipsy? [9]	Chi del gitano i giorni abbella?
Who never, never fails him?	Chi, chi i giorni abbella?
The zingarella!	La zingarella!

MEN
(to the women, resting briefly from their work)

Bring round the wine-jug; for wine revives	Versami un tratto; lena e corraggio
Our strength and spirits too, and brings new courage.	Il corpo e a l'anima traggon dal bere.

(The women pour them wine in rustic cups.)

ALL

See how the nectar that flows in our tankards	Oh guarda, guarda! del sole un raggio
Sparkles and shines like a miser's treasure!	Brilla più vivido nel tuo bicchiere!
More work is waiting!	All'opra, all'opra ...
Who cheers the days of the poor roving gipsy?	Chi del gitano i giorni abbella?
Who never, never fails him?	Chi, chi i giorni abella?
The zingarella!	La zingarella!

AZUCENA
(As she sings, the Gipsies gather around her.)

Fierce flames are raging! – see how the noisy crowd [10]	Stride la vampa! – la folla indomita
Surges around her, eager for slaughter.	Corre a quel foco – lieta in sembianza;
Yells of derision rise up from every side:	Urli di gioia – intorno echeggiano:
Here comes the gipsy, led to the torture!	Cinta si sgherri – donna s'avanza!
Dark fires are shining in all those hateful eyes,	Sinistra splende – sui volti orribili
While through the smoke flames are rising to scorch the skies!	La tetra fiamma – che s'alza al ciel!
Fierce flames are raging! There stands the sacrifice,	Stride la vampa! – giunge la vittima
Clad in her black robe, barefoot and haggard!	Nero-vestita, – discinta e scalza!
Howls of rejoicing greet her last agony;	Grido feroce – di morte levasi;
Hark! How they echo, far down the valley!	L'eco il ripete – di balza in balza!
Dark fires are shining in all those hateful eyes,	Sinistra splende – sui volti orribili
While through the smoke flames are rising to scorch the skies!	La tetra fiamma – che s'alza al ciel!

You sing a tragic song.   Mesta è la tua canzon!

AZUCENA

       Yet no more tragic   Del pari mesta
Than that awful deed of horror   Che la storia funesta
Which has given my song its story.   Da cui tragge argomento!
(She turns her head towards Manrico and murmurs softly:)
Avenge my death! Avenge my death!   Mi vendica! . . . mi vendica!

MANRICO

        (Again   (L'arcana
Those mysterious words!)   Parola ognor!)

OLD GIPSY

   It's time that we were starting   Compagni, avanza il giorno:
Our daily search for food. Come on! Let's   A procacciarci un pan, su, su! . . . scendiamo
all try
Our luck along the valley.   Per le propinque ville.

MEN

     You lead us.   Andiamo.
(They carefully stow their tools in their bags.)

WOMEN

We'll follow.   Andiamo.

(They set off down the hill in a throng. From time to time they can be heard singing further and further away.)

GIPSIES

Who cheers the days of the poor roving   Chi del gitano i giorni abbella?
  gipsy?
Who never fails him?   Chi, chi i giorni abbella?
The zingarella!   La zingarella!

No. 5. Recitative and Narrative

MANRICO
(getting up)

We're alone here. Now tell me   Soli or siamo; deh, narra
More about that sad story!   Quella storià funesta.

AZUCENA

     So, you've not heard it   E tu la ignori,
Before? But since your boyhood, wars and   Tu pur? . . . Ma, giovinetto, i passi tuoi
battles
Have always kept you   D'ambizion lo sprone
Far from your people. The tale concerns   Lungi traea! . . . Dell'ava il fine acerbo
the death
Of my own mother . . . She was caught by a   È quest'istoria . . . La incolpò superbo
certain
Count and accused of witchcraft. When   Conte di malefizio, onde apparia.
his son lay dying,
He said that she'd bewitched him. That   Colto un bambin suo figlio . . . Essa bruciata
cruel man
Condemned her to perish in torment!   Venne ov'arde quel foco!

MANRICO
(drawing back in horror from the fire)

    Ill-fated woman!   Ahi! sciagurata!

AZUCENA

They brought her, fettered and powerless [11] Condotta ell'era in ceppi al suo destin
to suffer her cruel sentence!   tremendo!
My child safe on my shoulder, I followed at   Col figlio sulle braccia, io la seguia
a distance.   piangendo.

In vain I tried to approach her, the crowd
  proved too fierce and pressing . . .
In vain she tried to break away and give me
  her blessing.
Guards shouted maledictions, their blows
  rained down around her,
They brought her to that fearful place,
  there to the stake they bound her!
At last in her dying anguish 'Avenge my
  death', she cried.
Those words that will not leave me, remind
  me still how she died.

Infino ad essa un varco tentai, ma invano,
  aprirmi . . .
Invan tentò la misera fermarsi e benedirmi!

Che, fra bestemmie oscene, pungendola coi
  ferri,
Al rogo la cacciavano gli scellerati sgherri! . . .

Allor, con tronco accento . . . Mi vendica! . . .
  sclamò.
Quel detto un'eco eterna in questo cor
  lasciò.

MANRICO

Did you avenge her?

La vendicasti?

AZUCENA

I stole the child from his father's palace,
And took him down there with me . . . I
  soon had the fire relighted.

Il figlio giunsi a rapir del Conte:
Lo trascinai qui meco . . . Le fiamme
  ardean già pronte.

MANRICO
(*in horror*)

The fire! Oh God! You mean it?

Le fiamme! . . . Oh ciel! . . . tu forse?

AZUCENA

That helpless infant was crying . . .
I felt my heart warm towards him, thoughts
  of vengeance were dying . . .
That moment I saw my error, memories
  came to haunt me.
I beheld those phantoms rise up again
  before me!
The soldiers . . . there stood my mother . . .
  still writhing in her torment . . .
Barefoot and haggard . . . that message,
  her dying message, I heard it . . .
'Avenge my death!' . . . My fingers con-
  vulsed with terror . . . snatched
Up that tiny child . . . I saw that inferno,
  there I threw him!
When I regained my senses I felt new life
  returning;
The raging fire still faced me, there was the
  victim burning!
But when I looked around me, I saw the
  child I'd stolen
Still lying there beside me . . .

Ei distruggeasi in pianto . . .
Io mi sentiva il core dilaniato, infranto! . . .

Quand'ecco agli egri spirti, come in un
  sogno, apparve
La vision ferale di spaventose larve!

Gli sgherri ed il supplizio! . . . la madre
  smorta in volto . . .
Scalza, discinta! . . . il grido, il noto grido
  ascolto . . .
"Mi vendica! . . . " La mano convulsa
  stendo . . . stringo
La vittima . . . nel foco la traggo, la
  sospingo!
Cessa il fatal delirio . . . l'orrida scena
  fugge . . .
La fiamma sol divampa, e la sua preda
  strugge!
Pur volgo intorno il guardo e innanzi a me
  vegg'io
Dell'empio Conte il figlio! . . .

MANRICO

There, beside you? Ah!

Ah, che dici?

AZUCENA

It was my own child,
My child that I had murdered!

Il figlio mio,
Mio figlio avea bruciato!

MANRICO

Your own child!

Quale orror!

AZUCENA

Ah! My own child, my own child,
It was my own child,
My only child that I had murdered.

Ah! Mio figlio, mio figlio,
Il figlio mio,
Il figlio mio avea bruciato!

MANRICO

Heaven above forgive your crime.
Oh God! Say no more!

Quale orror! oh quale orror!
Orror! Quale orror!

These bitter memories that haunt me still make my blood run cold!

Sul capo mio le chiome sento drizzarsi ancor!

Azucena falls back in exhaustion; Manrico is struck dumb with shock and horror. There is a moment of silence. / No. 6. Recitative and Duet

MANRICO

If your child perished, who was my mother? Who am I?

Non son tuo figlio! E chi son io? chi dunque?

AZUCENA
(*anxiously trying to correct her mistake*)

You are my own son!

Tu sei mio figlio!

MANRICO

And yet, this story ...

Eppure dicesti ...

AZUCENA

The story
Means nothing! When I recall that morning my mother
Perished, dark shadows cloud my memory, and my lips
Speak of stupid thoughts and fancies. Tell me,
Have I not always been a loving mother?

Ah! ... forse? ...
Che vuoi! ... quando al pensier s'affaccia il truce
Caso, lo spirto intenebrato pone

Stolte parole sul mio labbro ... Madre,

Tenera madre non m'avesti ognora?

MANRICO

None could deny it.

Potrei negarlo?

AZUCENA

And if you are still living,
Who saved you? At midnight, after your defeat
Before Pelilla, where they said
You'd died in the struggle, did I not
Come to seek you for burial? When I found you there,
And saw that you still breathed, were you not
Recalled to life through my devotion? For months
I watched here beside you and healed the wounds from which
You were bleeding!

A me, se vivi ancora,
Nol dei? Notturna, nei pugnati campi

Di Pelilla, ove spento
Fama ti disse, a darti
Sepoltura non mossi? La fuggente

Aura vital non iscovri, nel seno

Non t'arrestò materno affetto? E quante

Cure non spesi a risanar le tante

Ferite! ...

MANRICO
(*with noble pride*)

Wounds I suffered in the battle ...
They brought me no dishonour, for when our troops
Were all defeated, I alone faced
The foe with none to help me! ... At last that vile Count
Luna's men had me surrounded; they triumphed,
I fell, fell like a soldier!

Che portai nel di fatale ...
Ma tutte qui, nel petto! ... Io sol, fra mille

Già sbandati, al nemico
Volgendo ancor la faccia! ... Il rio di Luna
Su me piombò col suo drappello; io caddi!

Però da forte io caddi!

AZUCENA

There's your reward
For the mercy that you showed him
The night you overpowered him,
Then let him escape! ... What could have blinded you?
Why did your courage fail you?
You spared his life!

Ecco mercede
Ai giorni, che l'infame
Nel singolar certame
Ebbe salvi da te! ... Qual t'accecava

Strana pietà per esso?
Strana pietà!

O mother, I hardly know how to answer! | Oh madre! . . . Non saprei dirlo a me stesso!

As we struggled he stumbled before me, [12] Mal reggendo all'aspro assalto,
Shamed and humbled, he lay at my mercy: Ei già tocco il suolo avea;
In the starlight my sword flashed above me,   Balenava il colpo in alto
Poised to strike him dead that moment . . .   Che trafiggerlo dovea . . .
Then some unknown power detained me,   Quando arresta un moto arcano,
Some mysterious voice restrained me,   Nel discender, questa mano . . .
And I shuddered, my blood ran cold as ice,   Le mie fibre acuto gelo
I heard a strange command,   Fa repente abbrividir!
As if an angel came from Heaven above   Mentre un grido vien dal cielo,
And murmured, 'Stay your hand!'   Che mi dice: non ferir!

Yet no angel voice from Heaven [13] Ma nell'alma dell'ingrato
Shows concern for your survival,   Non parlò del ciel un detto!
And if fate again should lead you   Oh! se ancor ti spinge il fato
Into combat with your rival,   A pugnar col maledetto,
Show him no mercy, never betray me,   Compi, o figlio, qual d'un Dio,
Always remember you must obey me!   Compi allora il cenno mio!
Have no pity, plunge this weapon   Sino all'elsa questa lama
Deep into the traitor's heart.   Vibra, immergi all'empio in cor.
Show him no mercy and have no remorse,   Vibra, immergi all'empio in cor!
Strike and kill him, I command you;   Sino all'elsa questa lama,
Show no mercy, plunge your sword into   Questa lama vibra, immergi all'empio in
  his heart,   core,
Plunge your sword into his heart.   Vibra, immergi all'empio in cor.

Yes, I swear it, I'll not spare him,   Si, lo giuro, questa lama
And my sword shall find his heart.   Scenderà dell'empio in cor.
(A long horn-call is heard.)
  That is our signal, it comes from Ruiz.   L'usato messo Ruiz invia!
I'll answer.   Forse . . .

(He blows on the horn which he wears slung over his shoulder.)

  'Avenge my death!'   Mi vendica!

(She sits absorbed, almost unconscious of what now occurs.)

Scene Two. *Messenger and the above.*

    Tell me your news.   Inoltra il piè.
How goes the battle, what is the outcome?   Guerresco evento, dimmi, seguia?

This secret letter will tell you all.   Risponda il foglio che reco a te.

"Our men have captured Castellar; by   "In nostra possa è Castellor; ne déi
  order
Of the Prince you are charged   Tu, per cenno del prence,
With its defence. When you receive this,   Vigilar le difese. Ove ti è dato,
Come as quickly as you can. This very   Affrettati a venir . . . Giunta la sera,
  evening
Leonora, believing you to be dead,   Tratta in inganno di tua morte al grido,
Will take the veil in the neighbouring   Nel vicin chiostro della croce il velo
Convent of the Holy Cross."   Cingerà Leonora."
(crying out in sorrow)
    My Leonora!   Oh giusto cielo!

(What's happening?)   (Che fia!)

MANRICO
(to the messenger)

Go quickly down to the valley,	Veloce scendi la balza,
See that a horse is ready for me.	Ed un cavallo a me provvedi ...

MESSENGER

Yes!	Corro ...

AZUCENA
(interrupting)

Manrico!	Manrico!

MANRICO

Don't lose a moment,	Il tempo incalza ...
Hurry, and tell them to meet me below there.	Vola, m'aspetta del colle ai piedi?

(The messenger rushes out.)

AZUCENA

Manrico, you're leaving?	E speri, e vuoi?

MANRICO

(If I stay, I lose her ...	(Perderla? ... Oh ambascia! ...
Lose Leonora! ...)	Perder quell'angelo? ...)

AZUCENA

(He must be mad!)	(È fuor di sè!)

MANRICO
(putting on his helmet and snatching up his cloak)

Goodbye!	Addio ...

AZUCENA

No, stay here, listen ...	No ... ferma ... odi ...

MANRICO

I cannot ...	Mi lascia ...

AZUCENA
(asserting her authority)

Stay here: your mother speaks to you!	Ferma ... Son io che parlo a te!
You are still too weak to venture	[14] Perigliarti ancor languente
On a lonely path full of danger!	Per cammin selvaggio ed ermo!
All those wounds of yours, you madman,	La ferite vuoi, demente,
Once again may wrack you with fever.	Riaprir del petto infermo?
No, I cannot let you suffer,	No, soffrirlo non poss'io ...
You, my life, my very being!	Il tuo sangue è sangue mio! ...
Every drop of blood you shed	Ogni stilla che ne versi
Comes from this poor heart of mine!	Tu la spremi dal mio cor!

MANRICO

If I stay a moment longer,	[15] Un momento può involarmi
Then I lose my love, my treasure!	Il mio ben, la mia speranza! ...
Neither earth nor Heaven has power	No, che basti ad arrestarmi
To divert me from my purpose!	Terra e ciel non han possanza ...

AZUCENA

Manrico!	Demente!

MANRICO

Do not keep me, for I must leave you;	Ah! ... mi sgombra, o madre, i passi ...
If I stayed my tears would grieve you!	Guai per te s'io qui restassi! ...
You would see me die before you	Tu vedresti a' piedi tuoi
Of a coward's broken heart!	Spento il figlio di dolor!

(As he leaves, Azucena tries vainly to hold him back.)

Scene Three. *The cloister of a convent near Castellar. In the background are trees. It is night. The Count, Ferrando and a few of the Count's Retainers creep cautiously in, wrapped in their cloaks. / No. 7. Recitative and Aria*

COUNT

No sound of chanting; all those pious women	Tutto è deserto, nè per l'aura ancora
Have not yet begun their praying . . .	Suona l'usato carme . . .
I'm here in time then!	In tempo io giungo!

FERRANDO

This mad adventure still may prove	Ardita opra, o Signore,
Too dangerous.	Imprendi.

COUNT

I know it, yet tortured by my passion,	Ardita, e qual furente amore
Spurred on by injured pride,	Ed irritato orgoglio
My heart knows no fear. With Manrico dead, there seemed	Chiesero a me. Spento il rival, caduto
To be nothing remaining to thwart my wishes;	Ogni ostacol sembrava a' miei desiri;
But now she's raised another barrier between us . . .	Novello e più possente ella ne appresta . . .
The cloister! No, no! No-one else	L'altare! Ah no . . . non fia
Shall claim Leonora! She is mine, I swear it!	D'altri Leonora! . . . Leonora è mia.

All the stars that shine above me	[16] Il balen del suo sorriso
Cannot rival her celestial radiance;	D'una stella vince il raggio!
All her smiles whose charms delight me	Il fulgor del suo bel viso
Give me new courage in her presence!	Novo infonde in me coraggio! . . .
May the love, the love that I bear her,	Ah! l'amor, l'amore ond'ardo
Speak and bid her fears all depart!	Le favelli in mio favor! . . .
May the starshine of her glances	Sperda il sole d'un suo sguardo
Calm this tempest in my heart.	La tempesta del mio cor.

(The convent bells ring out.)

The signal! . . . Oh God!	Qual suono! . . . oh ciel! . . .

FERRANDO

That bell means	La squilla
They're coming to the chapel.	Vicino il rito annunzia!

COUNT

Before she reaches	Ah! pria che giunga
The altar we must seize her!	All'altar . . . si rapisca! . . .

FERRANDO

Be careful!	Ah bada!

COUNT

Silence,	Taci! . . .
I tell you! Obey me! Hide yourselves and keep out	Non odi? . . . andate . . . di quei faggi all'ombra
Of sight for now.	Celatevi . . .

(Ferrando and the other Retainers retire.)

Leonora	Ah! fra poco
Soon will be mine! Oh, how that thought inflames me!	Mia diverrà . . . Tutto m'investe un foco!

(He anxiously scans the direction from which Leonora is to enter while Ferrando and the Retainers repeat sottovoce:)

FERRANDO, RETAINERS

The hour has come, no more delay,	[17] Ardir! . . . andiam, . . . celiamoci
We'll hide away . . . no more delay!	Fra l'ombre . . . nel mister!
The hour has come, be silent all!	Ardir! . . . andiam, . . . silenzio!
My lord is here, and we obey!	Si compia il suo voler! ardir!
Now we know the hour has come,	Ah, silenzio ardir, ardir
We'll hide ourselves like shadows in the night.	Celiamozi fra l'ombre, nel mister.
The hour has come and we obey.	Ardir, andiam, ardir, andiam!

57

COUNT
(seized with passion)

My hour of joy approaches,	[18] Per me, ora fatale,
And how that thought elates me;	I tuoi momenti affretta:
The bliss that here awaits me,	La gioia che m'aspetta
No mortal man has known!	Gioia mortal non è! . . .
Though Heaven is now my rival,	Invano un Dio rivale
The cloister shall not claim her,	S'oppone all'amor mio;
Not God Himself shall gain her,	Non può nemmeno un Dio,
For she is mine alone!	Donna, rapirti a me!
Not even God in Heaven above me	Non può nemmen, nemmen un Dio
Can rob me now of all I prize.	O donna rapirti a me,
She's mine and mine alone!	Rapirti a me, rapirti a me

He retires slowly, concealing himself amongst the trees with the Retainers / No. 8. Finale

CHORUS OF NUNS
(off-stage)

Here in this world of sorrow,	[19] Ah! . . . se l'error t'ingombra,
Daughter of Eve, remember,	O figlia d'Eva, i rai,
Death's solemn hour will show you	Presso a morir, vedrai
All earthly joys are vain,	Che un'ombra, un sogno fu,
Life is an empty shadow,	Anzi del sogno un'ombra
Nothing but dreams remain!	La speme di quaggiù!
Come, leave the world for ever,	Vieni e t'asconda il velo
Put on the veil we offer,	Ad ogni sguardo umano!
Here you will find seclusion,	Aura o pensier mondano
Here you will find release.	Qui vivo più non è.
Come, turn your eyes to Heaven,	Al ciel ti volgi e il cielo
Heaven will give you peace.	Si schiuderà per te.

Scene Four. *Leonora with female companions. Inez, then the Count, Ferrando, Retainers and finally Manrico.*

LEONORA

But why this weeping?	Perchè piangete?

INEZ

Leonora,	Ah! . . . dunque
You now leave us for ever!	Tu per sempre ne lasci!

LEONORA

Faithful companions,	O dolci amiche,
No comfort, no earthly pleasure, no joy is left me,	Un riso, una speranza, un fior la terra
Since he is dead. I turn my eyes	Non ha per me! Degg'io
To our Lord, for He alone can comfort	Volgermi a Quel che degli afflitti è solo
My sorrow: then after prayer and humble penance	Sostegno e dopo i penitenti giorni
I may implore Him one day to re-unite me	Può fra gli eletti al mio perduto bene
With my loved one on high! So weep no longer,	Ricongiungermi un dì! . . . Tergete i rai
Lead the way to the altar.	E guidatemi all'ara!

(She turns to go.)

COUNT
(bursting in)

No . . . Stay here!	No, giammai! . . .

INEZ AND WOMEN

The Count!	Il Conte!

LEONORA

Can you dare?	Giusto ciel!

COUNT

As my own bride	Per te non havvi
You shall stand before the altar.	Che l'ara d'imeneo.

NUNS

What impious language!   Cotanto ardia . . .

LEONORA

You dare profane the cloister?   Insano! . . . E qui venisti?

COUNT

I come to claim you.   A farti mia.

(*With these words, he rushes to seize Leonora but, like a ghost rising from the ground, Manrico appears between him and his victim. All exclaim.*)

LEONORA

Oh can it be? Can I believe	[20] E deggio . . . e posso crederlo?
I see you here beside me?	Ti veggo a me d'accanto!
Is this a dream, a fantasy,	È questo un sogno, un'estasi,
A magic spell that binds me?	Un sovrumano incanto?
My heart can hardly bear this joy	Non regge a tanto giubilo
That here to me is given!	Rapito, il cor sorpreso!
Have you come down from Heaven,	Sei tu dal ciel disceso,
Or am I there by your side?	O in ciel son io con te?
My heart dare not believe this joy:	È questo un sogno, un estasi,
Is this a dream of love?	Un sogno, un estasi . . .

COUNT

So now the dead return again	Dunque gli estinti lasciano
From Hell's infernal regions!	Di morte il regno eterno;
Or can it be that Satan	A danno mio rinunzia
Rejects you from his legions?	Le prede sue l'inferno!
If you still live and life be dear,	Ma se non mai si fransero
And life be dear to think on,	De' giorni tuoi gli stami,
You must forget this woman,	Se vivi e viver brami,
And never cross my path again.	Fuggi da lei, da me!

MANRICO

Neither from Heaven nor Hell have I	Né m'ebbe il ciel, né l'orrido
Come back to spoil your pleasure.	Varco infernal sentiero . . .
Your hired assassins thought that they	Infami sgherri vibrano
Had killed me at Pelilla!	Mortali colpi, è vero!
Fiercer and fiercer grew the fight,	Potenza irresistibile
Though you had me surrounded,	Hanno de' fiumi l'onde!
The traitors were confounded,	Magli empi un Dio confonde!
For kindly Heaven sent me aid!	Quel Dio soccorse a me.

INEZ AND WOMEN
(*to Leonora*)

Now gracious Heaven, in whom you trusted,	Il cielo in cui fidasti
Sends you aid in this sad hour.	Pietade avea di te,
Our Lord has heard your prayer.	Pietade avea di te.

FERRANDO, RETAINERS
(*to the Count*)

You have defied your fortune,	Tu col destin contrasti,
And the might of Heaven above!	Suo difensore egli è.
But all in vain, for	Ah col destin contrasti,
her defender is at hand!	Suo difensore egli e.

Scene Five. *Ruiz with a long Troupe of armed followers, and with the above.*

RUIZ

Long live Urgel!   Urgel viva!

MANRICO

My friends, you are welcome!   Miei prodi guerrieri!

RUIZ

Follow!   Vieni . . .

MANRICO
(to Leonora)

Come, Leonora.   Donna, mi segui.

COUNT
(opposing him)

Would you cheat me? . . .   E tu speri?

LEONORA

Ah!   Ah!

MANRICO
(to the Count)

Stand back there . . .   T'arresta . . .

COUNT
(drawing his sword)

        Of my own rightful prize!   Involarmi costei!
No!   No!

RUIZ, SOLDIERS
(to the Count)

He's raving!   Vaneggi!

FERRANDO, SOLDIERS

        Be careful, my lord!   Che tenti, Signor?

(Ruiz's men disarm the Count.)

COUNT
(his tone and his gestures indicating maniacal rage)

Rage has driven me mad with desire!   Di ragione ogni lume perdei!

LEONORA

(How he scares me . . . terrifies me . . . Ah!)   (M'atterrisce . . . ah!)

COUNT

        And the torments of Hell   Ho le furie nel cor!
Will for ever be mine.   Ho le furie nel cor!

MANRICO

May you suffer, yes, in grief and despair.   Fia supplizio la vita per te.

RUIZ, SOLDIERS
(to Manrico)

Follow! For you will be safe in our care.   Vieni la sorte sorride pote.

FERRANDO, RETAINERS
(to the Count)

Leave her! For brave men must sometimes   Cedi; or ceder viltade non e.
forbear.

(Manrico drags Leonora after him; the Count is driven back; the women flee into the convent. The curtain falls quickly.)

Part Three: The Gipsy's Son

Scene One. *A camp. To the right, the Count di Luna's tent with a banner floating above it, denoting his supreme command. In the distance rise the towers of Castellar. Soldiers on sentry-duty all around; some are playing games, others are polishing their armour, others pacing up and down; then Ferrando, coming out of the Count's tent. / No. 9. Chorus of Soldiers*

SOME SOLDIERS

Though today we take our leisure,	[21] Or co'dadi, ma fra poco
Dawn will bring a sterner pleasure.	Giocherem ben altro gioco.

OTHERS

Swords that now are bright and shining	Quest'acciar, dal sangue or terso,
Will have tasted blood by morning!	Fia di sangue in breve asperso!

(A large contingent of bowmen crosses the camp.)

FIRST GROUP

Our reserves have come to join us.	Il soccorso dimandato!

OTHERS

They have come from near and far!	Han l'aspetto del valor!

ALL

We'll soon start the battle raging	Più l'assalto ritardato
Round the walls of Castellar.	Or non fia di Castellor.
At dawn we'll be there.	No, no, non fia più.

FERRANDO

Here are your orders; our noble captain commands	Sì, prodi amici, al dì novello è mente
That at break of day we make	Del capitan la rocca
An assault on the fortress.	Investir d'ogni parte.
When Castellar is taken	Colà pingue bottino
Rich plunder shall be yours, beyond believing.	Certezza è rinvenir più che speranza.
So courage, tomorrow!	Sì vinca; è nostro.

ALL

Lead us on, we follow!	Tu c'inviti a danza!
Let all the trumpets set echoes replying	[22] Squilli, echeggi la tromba guerriera,
When they summon us to battle and to plunder.	Chiami all'armi, alla pugna, all'assalto;
High on the walls let our banners be flying,	Fia domani la nostra bandiera
While our guns rage and roar like the thunder.	Di quei merli piantata sull'alto.
Never before has our triumph looked brighter,	No, giammai non sorrise vittoria
Nor our hope of success so assured!	Di più liete speranze finor! . . .
Booty and treasure now wait for us yonder,	Ivi l'util ci aspetta e la gloria,
Fame and glory shall be our reward.	Ivi opimi la preda e l'onor.
Fortune smiles on us all, we obey duty's call,	Ivi l'util ci aspetta e la gloria,
Fame and glory tomorrow shall be our reward.	Ivi opimi la preda e l'onor.

(They disperse.*)

---

* Verdi composed a ballet of four 'divertissements', to be inserted at this point, for the Opéra de Paris, in 1857, as follows: A group of gipsy dancers arrive and entertain the soldiers with dances: 1. Pas de Bohémiens, Gitanella, Ensemble; 2. Seviliana, la Vivandière, Echo de la Vivandière, Echo du Soldat; 3. La Bohémienne, Echo de la Bohémienne, Solo de la Bohémienne; 4. Galop, Apres la danse.

Scene Two. *The Count. He comes out of his tent and looks grimly towards Castellar.* / *No. 10. Recitative and Trio*

COUNT

She's in my rival's arms! That thought torments me,	In braccio al mio rival! Questo pensiero
It pursues me like some fiend of Hell.	Come persecutor demone ovunque
I cannot escape it. She's in my rival's arms . . . Tomorrow	M'insegue! . . . In braccio al mio rival! . . . Ma corro,
In the pale light of morning,	Sorta appena l'aurora,
They part, and part for ever. O Leonora!	Io corro a separarvi . . . Oh Leonora!

(Noise of an uproar.)

Scene Three. *Ferrando and the above.*

COUNT

What news?	Che fu?

FERRANDO

A gipsy woman	Dappresso il campo
Has been hanging around the camp today. As soon	S'aggirava una zingara: sorpresa
As she knew we were suspicious,	Da' nostri esploratori,
She tried to evade us; the soldiers thought the gipsy	Si volse in fuga; essi, a ragion temendo
Was a spy sent by those traitors . . .	Una spianella trista,
They gave chase.	L'inseguir . . .

COUNT

Then what happened?	Fu raggiunta?

FERRANDO

They caught her.	È presa.

COUNT

You've seen Her then?	Vista L'hai tu?

FERRANDO

No, but the leader Of her escort gave me That message.	No; della scorta Il condottier m'apprese L'evento.

COUNT

Here she comes.	Eccola.

(The uproar is heard closer at hand.)

Scene Four. *The above, Azucena with bound hands, dragged in by the Guards, and a troop of other soldiers.*

SCOUTS

Get on, you gipsy, get on there . . .	Innanzi, o strega, innanzi . . .

AZUCENA

Have mercy! Let me go now, hard-hearted villains!	Aita! . . . Mi lasciate . . . Ah: furibondi,
What harm have I done?	Che mal fec'io?

COUNT

Come forward . . .	S'appressi.

(Azucena is dragged before the Count.)

Reply, I charge you, And do not tell me lies.	A me rispondi E trema dal mentir!

AZUCENA

Speak then.	Chiedi!

COUNT

Where are you going?   Ove vai?

AZUCENA

Who knows?   Nol so.

COUNT

Answer!   Che? . . .

AZUCENA

     Every gipsy is accustomed   D'una zingara è costume
To abide where she pleases,   Mover senza disegno
In every land a stranger,   Il passo vagabondo,
Her roof the open sky, the whole world her   Ed è suo tetto il ciel, sua patria il mondo.
  country.

COUNT

Where've you come from?   E vieni?

AZUCENA

     From Biscaya; deep in the wild,   Da Biscaglia, ove finora
Barren mountains of that region I found a   Lo sterili montagne ebbi a ricetto!
  refuge.

COUNT

(From Biscaya!)   (Da Biscaglia!)

FERRANDO

   (Biscaya! That is suspicious!)   (Che intesi! . . . O qual sospetto!)

AZUCENA

Though my life was poor and lowly,   [23] Giorni poveri vivea,
I was happy and contented;   Pur contenta del mio stato:
But, alas! my son has left me   Sola speme un figlio avea . . .
All alone and unprotected.   Mi lasciò! . . . m'oblia, l'ingrato!
On I go, sad and forsaken,   Io, deserta, vado errando
Searching paths he may have taken,   Di quel figlio ricercando,
Every day I hope to find him,   Di quel figlio che al mio core
All my grief he cannot know.   Pene orribili costò! . . .
Fonder love than I still bear him,   Qual per esso provo amore
No mother here on earth could show.   Madre in terra non provò!

FERRANDO

(There's a likeness!)   (Il suo volto!)

COUNT

     So, you've lived   Di', traesti
For many years there in Biscaya?   Lunga etade tra quei monti?

AZUCENA

Many years.   Lunga, sì.

COUNT

     Would you remember   Rammenteresti
Twenty years ago, a child of noble family   Un fanciul, prole di conti,
Was abducted from his palace,   Involato al suo castello,
And was taken to those same mountains?   Son tre lustri, e tratto quivi?

AZUCENA

Who are you, tell me . . . who?   E tu, parla . . . sei? . . .

COUNT

    The brother   Fratello
Of that infant.   Del rapito.

AZUCENA

   (Ah!)   (Ah!)

FERRANDO
(perceiving Azucena's ill-concealed terror)

(Yes!)   (Sì!)

COUNT

So you can   Ne udivi
Tell me nothing?   Mai novella?

AZUCENA

Nothing! No! Allow me   Io? ... No ... Concedi
To continue on my journey.   Che del figlio l'orme io scopra.

FERRANDO

Keep her prisoner!   Resta, iniqua ...

AZUCENA

(O God!)   (Ohimè! ...)

FERRANDO

For here   Tu vedi
At last we've caught the wretch who did   Chi l'infame, orribil opra
that
Cruel murder ...   Commettea ...

COUNT

You're certain!   Finisci.

FERRANDO

I'm certain!   È dessa.

AZUCENA
(softly to Ferrando)

(Silence!)   (Taci!)

FERRANDO

There stands the fiend who killed   È dessa che il bambino
Your brother!   Arse!

COUNT

You murderess!   Ah! perfida!

SOLDIERS

She's that gipsy!   Ella stessa!

AZUCENA

You are lying ...   Ei mentisce ...

COUNT

But this time you   Al tuo destino
Shall not escape us.   Or non fuggi.

AZUCENA

Ah!   Deh! ...

COUNT

Now bind her   Quei nodi
Arms securely.   Più stringete.

(The Soldiers do so.)

AZUCENA

Have pity, have pity!   Oh! Dio! ... Oh! Dio! ...

SOLDIERS

Howl, you witch!   Urla pur!

AZUCENA
(in desperation)

My son, where are you?	E tu non vieni,
Oh Manrico, come and help me,	O Manrico, o figlio mio? ...
Come and save me, your most	Non soccorri all'infelice
Unhappy mother!	Madre tua?

COUNT

You're Manrico's gipsy mother?   Di Manrico genitrice!

FERRANDO

Kill her!   Trema! ...

COUNT

A prisoner in my power! What triumph!   Oh sorte! ... in mio poter!

AZUCENA

Ah! Release me from these cruel bonds,	[24]	Deh, rallentate, o barbari,
Have mercy, I implore you,		Le acerbe mie ritorte ...
Have pity on my torment,		Questo crudel martirio
Or I shall die before you!		E prolungata morte! ...
You hateful son, more evil		D'iniquo genitore
Than your hated father,		Empio figliuol peggiore,
Tyrant! Beware, for God protects the poor;		Trema! ... v'è Dio pei miseri,
His vengeance will fall upon you all.		E Dio ti punirà!

COUNT

The treacherous Manrico	[25]	Tua prole, o turpe zingara,
Is your son, you crazy gipsy,		Colui, quel traditore? ...
And so with every pang you suffer		Potrò col tuo supplizio
I wound him to the heart!		Ferirlo in mezzo al cor!
Your capture proves a blessing,		Gioia m'innonda il petto,
Bringing joy past all expressing,		Cui non esprime il detto! ...
For by my brother's death I swear,		Meco il fraterno cenere
I'll have my vengeance at last.		Piena vendetta avrà!

FERRANDO, SOLDIERS

You murderous witch, your time has come,	Infame pira sorgere,
For you a pyre will soon be burning.	Ah, sì, vedrai tra poco ...
And after that there's Hell-fire,	Nè solo tuo supplizio
From whence there's no returning!	Sarà terreno foco! ...
For you the fires are burning,	Le vampe dell'inferno
From Hell there's no returning,	A te fian rogo eterno;
And you cannot escape them!	Ivi penare ed ardere
In never-ending agony	L'anima tua dovrà!
Your soul shall burn for evermore!	Ivi penar, penar ed ardere!

(At a signal from the Count, the Soldiers drag off Azucena. The Count withdraws into his tent, followed by Ferrando.)

Scene Five. *A room next to the chapel in Castellar, with a balcony in the background. Manrico, Leonora and Ruiz./ No. 11. Recitative and Aria*

LEONORA

But what mean all these sounds of war around us?   Quale d'armi fragor poc'anzi intesi?

MANRICO

We are in danger, I can	Alto è il periglio! vano
No longer keep it secret!	Dissimularlo fora!
For at the break of day	Alla novella aurora
Luna's men will attack us.	Assaliti saremo! ...

LEONORA

Alas! What turmoil!   Ahimè! ... che dici? ...

MANRICO

Have no fear, for tomorrow	Ma de' nostri nemici
We shall triumph. Though	Avrem vittoria ... Pari
Our foe be brave and strong, we are	Abbiam al loro ardir, brando e
his equal.	coraggio! ...

(to Ruiz)

Go down, prepare for battle.	Tu va'; le belliche opre,
You yourself will give orders,	Nell'assenza mia breve, a te
until I follow.	commetto.
See all is ready.	Che nulla manchi! ...

(Exit Ruiz.)

Scene Six. *Manrico and Leonora.*

LEONORA

What unhappy shadows	Di qual tetra luce
Have come to cloud our marriage!	Il nostro imen risplende!

MANRICO

Come forget all these fancies,	Il presagio funesto,
Dear Leonora!	Deh, sperdi, o cara! ...

LEONORA

How can I?	E il posso?

MANRICO

Our love and our devotion	Amor ... sublime amore,
In time of danger will sustain and inspire	In tale istante ti favelli al core.
us.	

When holy church has blessed our love, [26]	Ah! si, ben mio; coll'essere
Our hearts will grieve no longer;	Io tuo, tu mia consorte,
A sterner faith will fire my soul,	Avrò più l'alma intrepida,
My arm will fight the stronger.	Il braccio avrò più forte;
But if within the book of fate	Ma pur se nella pagina
My name has been recorded,	De' miei destini è scritto
As one of those who fall today,	Ch'io resti fra le vittime
Alone and unrewarded,	Dal ferro ostil trafitto,
Then in that hour when death is near	Fra quegli estremi aneliti,
My thoughts to you will quickly fly.	A te il pensier verrà
Take heart, my love, and have no fear,	E solo in ciel precederti
We meet again on high.	La morte a me parrà!

(The organ is heard playing in the chapel.)

LEONORA, MANRICO

The sound of solemn harmony	L'onda de' suoni mistici
Tells all the joy of faithful love!	Pura discende al cor!
Here we shall gain the grace	Vieni; ci schiude il tempio
And blessing of Heaven above.	Gioie di casto amor.

(They are making their way joyfully into the chapel when Ruiz rushes in.)

RUIZ

Manrico!	Manrico?

MANRICO

Yes!	Che?

RUIZ

That gipsy there ...	La zingara,
Hurry, she's now their prisoner.	Vieni, tra ceppi mira ...

MANRICO

Their prisoner?	Oh Dio!

RUIZ

And Count di Luna's men	Per man de' barbari
Have made a fire to burn her.	Accesa è già la pira ...

66

MANRICO
(crossing to the balcony)

My strength has gone from every limb . . .　　Oh ciel! mie membra oscillano . . .
Darkness is closing round me!　　Nube mi copre il ciglio!

LEONORA

You're trembling!　　Tu fremi!

MANRICO

　　Leonora! . . . Learn the truth.　　　　E il deggio! . . . Sappilo.
She is . . .　　Io son . . .

LEONORA

Well then?　　Chi mai?

MANRICO

　　My mother!　　　　Suo figlio! . . .
The villains! The thought of such a deed　　Ah! vili! . . . il rio spettacolo
Drives me nearly mad with fury!　　Quasi il respir m'invola . . .
Go out there, Ruiz, and call our men　　Raduna i nostri, affrettati . . .
To arms. Go! Go! Hurry! Hurry!　　Ruiz . . . va . . . va . . . torna . . . vola! . . .

(Exit Ruiz.)

That fierce inferno, her cruel sentence,　[27]　Di quella pira l'orrendo foco
Fire me with fever, set me aflame!　　tutte le fibre m'arse, avvampò
Ruffians repent this deed, or I'll have　　Empi spegnetela, o ch'io fra poco
　　vengeance!
Your blood shall wipe out insult and shame!　　Col sangue vostro la spegnorò . . .

(to Leonora)

(She loved me dearly, I'll not desert her;　　Era già figlio prima d'amarti,
All your entreaties, I must deny.)　　Non può frenarmi il tuo martir,
Ill-fated mother, snared by that traitor,　　Madre infelice, corro a salvarti,
I come to save you, save you or die.　　O teco almeno corro a morir!

LEONORA

I can no longer endure misfortune,　　Non reggo a colpi tanto funesti . . .
If you forsake me, then I shall die.　　Oh, quanto meglio saria morir!

(Re-enter Ruiz with Soldiers.)

RUIZ, SOLDIERS

Command us, command us! We all obey　　All'armi, all'armi! all'armi! all'armi!
　　your call.
To battle, to battle, may Heaven guard　　All'armi! all'armi! all'armi! all'armi
　　us all.
We all are ready to fight beside you,　　Ecco ne presti a pugnar teco, o teco la
　　to save her or die.　　　　morir.
Command us, we follow! Away to victory　　All'armi! all'armi! all'armi! all'armi!
　　and triumph!

(Exit Manrico in haste, followed by Ruiz and Soldiers; the clash of weapons and trumpets is heard off-stage.)

Part Four: The Torture

Scene One. *A wing of the Aliaferia Palace. At the corner is a tower, its windows guarded by iron bars. The night is very dark. Two muffled figures approach: they are Ruiz and Leonora. / No. 12. Recitative and Aria*

RUIZ
(softly)

We're there now; this is the fortress; here all the captured	Siam giunti; ecco la torre, ove di Stato
Rebels await their sentence. He is imprisoned there	Gemono i prigionieri . . . ah, l'infelice
In that tower!	Ivi fu tratto!

LEONORA

Ruiz, Leave me here. Have no fear for me, I beg you,	Vanne, Lasciami, nè timor di me ti prenda . . .
Perhaps I still may save him.	Salvarlo io potrò forse.

(Ruiz withdraws.)

Why fear for me? The poison here In this ring protects me.	Timor di me? . . . sicura, Presta è la mia difesa.

(She gazes intently at a ring on her right hand.)

The night's dark shadows Hide me; he does not know that I am watching,	In quest'oscura Notte ravvolta, presso a te son io,
That I am near him.You mournful Breezes that murmur round me,	E tu nol sai . . . Gemente Aura che intorno spiri,
In mercy tell him of all my grief and longing . . .	Deh, pietosa gli arreca i miei sospiri . . .
Breeze of the night go seek him,	[28] D'amor sull'ali rosee
Echo my tears and sighing;	Vanne, sospir dolente;
Go, tell the captive troubadour,	Del prigioniero misero
Love like mine is undying.	Conforta l'egra mente . . .
Bring hope and consolation	Com'aura di speranza
To cheer his desolation,	Aleggia in quella stanza:
Recall our treasured memories,	Lo desta alle memorie,
Our happy dreams of love.	Ai sogni dell'amor!
But here tonight he must never know	Ma deh! non dirgli, improvvido,
The torment in my heart.	Le pene del mio cor!

(The passing-bell is tolled.)

VOICES OFF-STAGE

Lord, have mercy upon a soul departing	[29] Miserere d'un'alma già vicina
For that abode from which there's no returning!	Alla partenza che non ha ritorno!
Lord, have mercy, and with Thy love sustain him,	Miserere di lei, bontà divina,
Grant that the fires of Hell may never claim him!	Preda non sia dell'infernal soggiorno!

LEONORA

That sound and those voices, that hymn for the dying,	[30] Quel suon, quelle preci solenni, funeste,
Re-echoes around these walls and chills me with fear!	Empiron quest'aere di cupo terror! . . .
It stifles my breathing, my courage is failing,	Contende l'ambascia, che tutta m'investe,
I know that his last hour on earth now is near!	Al labbro il respiro, i palpiti al cor!

(She stands absorbed in thought; after a few moments she starts, and is on the point of leaving, when a groan is heard from the tower, followed by a mournful sound; she stops.)

MANRICO
(from the tower)

Ah! When will death console me,	[32] Ah, che la morte ognora
When will he set me free?	È tarda nel venir
Life holds no pleasure for me!	A chi desia morir! . . .
Farewell, my love, my Leonora!	Addio, Leonora!

VOICES OFF-STAGE

Lord, have mercy upon a soul departing	Miserere d'un'alma già vicina
For that abode from which there's no returning.	Alla partenza che non ha ritorno!
Lord, have mercy, and with Thy love sustain him,	Miserere di lei, bontà divina,
Grant that the fires of Hell may never claim him!	Preda non sia dell'infernal soggiorno!
Miserere! Miserere!	Miserere! Miserere!

LEONORA

Now death is approaching that horrible tower	Sull'orrida torre, ahi! par che la morte
The sound of his beating wings is over my head,	Con ali di tenebre librando si va!
And for my beloved the gates of the prison	Ah! forse dischiuse gli fian queste porte
Will never be opened until he is dead!	Sol quando cadaver già freddo sarà!

MANRICO
(from the tower)

Faithful to vows we plighted,	Sconto col sangue mio
I meet my death today!	L'amor che posi in te!
Never forget me, pray!	Non ti scordar di me!
Farewell, my love, my Leonora!	Leonora, addio!

LEONORA

Could I, could I forget you? [32]	Di te, di te scordarmi!
I'm yours forever! Oh God have mercy!	Di te scordarmi! Sento mancarmi!
You will see that my devotion	Tu vedrai che amore in terra
Here on earth has known no equal.	Mai del mio non fu più forte;
Fate has yielded to its power;	Vinse il fato in aspra guerra,
Death itself shall not prevail,	Vincerà la stessa morte.
I myself will buy your freedom,	O col prezzo di mia vita
At the price of my poor life.	La tua vita salverò,
Should we not be at last re-united,	O con te per sempre unita
Then the grave itself will end the strife!	Nella tomba scenderò.

Scene Two. *A door opens; through it come the Count and some of his Retainers. Leonora withdraws.* / *No. 13. Recitative and Duet*

COUNT

You hear me? Bring the man down	Udiste? come albeggi,
At dawn and behead him, then light the pyre for his mother.	La scure al figlio ed alla madre il rogo.

(The Count's men enter the tower.)

Although I do perhaps abuse the power	Abuso forse quel poter che pieno
The Prince conferred upon me, love for that woman	In me trasmise il prence! A tal mi traggi,
Drives me to all this madness. And now I've lost her!	Donna per me funesta! . . . Ov'ella è mai?
We captured Castellar, but she herself	Ripreso Castellor, di lei contezza
Has escaped us. Our search was useless,	Non ebbi, e furo indarno
None of my spies has seen her.	Tante ricerche e tante! . . .
If I could only find her!	Ah! dove sei, crudele?

LEONORA
(coming forward)

Seek her no longer!	A te davante.

COUNT

Can this be . . . really . . . Leonora?	Qual voce! . . . come! . . . tu, donna?

LEONORA

No other!	Il vedi.

COUNT

What brings you here then?	A che venisti?

LEONORA

When he is doomed	Egli è già presso
To die tomorrow, how can you ask me?	All'ora estrema; e tu lo chiedi?

COUNT

You dare defy me?	Osar potresti? . . .

LEONORA

Yes, to implore you	Ah sì, per esso
To spare Manrico.	Pietà domando . . .

COUNT

Go! You are raving!	Che? tu deliri!
Ah! How could I spare my rival's life?	Ah! Io del rivale sentir pietà?

LEONORA

May Heaven move your heart to pity . . .	Clemente Nume a te l'ispiri . . .

COUNT

Not even Heaven can move me,	E sol vendetta mia Nume.
My God is one of vengeance.	Vendetta è sol mio Nume.
Go I say! Go I say!	Va! va! va! va! va! va!

LEONORA
(throwing herself in desperation at his feet)

Witness these bitter tears of mine,	[33] Mira, di acerbe lagrime
See all the grief I suffer;	Spargo al tuo piede un rio:
If this should fail to melt your heart,	Non basta il pianto? svenami,
Then take the sacrifice I offer . . .	Ti bevi il sangue mio . . .
Kill me then, let me die . . .	Svenami, svenami,
Let all your anger fall on me,	Calpesta il mio cadavere,
And pardon the Troubadour!	Ma salva il Trovator!

COUNT

Ah! Could he die a thousand deaths,	[34] Ah! dell'indegno rendere
I'd never be contented,	Vorrei peggior la sorte:
By all the pangs of Hell itself,	Fra mille atroci spasimi
I'd still have him tormented.	Centuplicar sua morte . . .
You love him and so my jealousy	Più l'ami, e più terribile
Now burns fiercer than before!	Divampa il mio furor!
You love him, and your devotion	Più l'ami, e più terribil
Condemns him for evermore.	Divampa il mio furor,
All your entreaties	E più terribile
Cannot save the Troubadour!	Divampa il mio furor.

(He tries to leave, but Leonora clings to him.)

LEONORA

Luna!	Conte . . .

COUNT

It's useless . . .	Nè cessi?

LEONORA

Mercy!	Grazia!

COUNT

No price on earth can buy	Prezzo non avvi alcuno
Your lover's freedom! Leave me now.	Ad ottenerla . . . scostati . . .

LEONORA

One price there is, one only . . .	Uno ve n'ha . . . sol uno! . . .
And that I offer.	Ed io te l'offro.

COUNT

What's the price	Spiegati,
You offer? Speak!	Qual prezzo, di'?

LEONORA
(holding out her hand to him in grief)

Myself!	Me stessa!

COUNT

What? Do you mean it?	Ciel! . . . tu dicesti?

LEONORA

I vow that I	E compiere
Will keep my solemn promise.	Saprò la mia promessa.

COUNT

Can I be dreaming?	È sogno il mio . . .

LEONORA

Now let me climb	Dischiudimi
the stairway to the tower,	La via fra quelle mura . . .
To tell him that he's free	Ch'ei m'oda . . . Che la vittima
And release him . . . then I'm yours.	Fugga, e son tua.

COUNT

You swear it?	Lo giura.

LEONORA

To God I swear it, He knows all	Lo giuro a Dio che l'anima
My innermost secrets.	Tutta mi vede!

COUNT

You there!	Olà!

(He runs to the tower gate. A guard appears; while the Count is whispering to him, Leonora takes the poison hidden in the ring.)

LEONORA

(A cold and lifeless body will	(M'avrai, ma fredda esanime
Await you.)	Spolgia.)

COUNT
(returning, to Leonora)

The man shall live!	Colui vivrà.

LEONORA
(She raises her eyes, which are veiled in tears of joy.)

(He lives! I cannot speak for joy.	[35] (Vivrà! . . . Contende il giubilo
To thank you, O Heavenly Father,	I detti a me, Signore . . .
This wildly beating heart of mine	Ma coi frequenti palpiti
Now tells you of my fervour!	Mercè ti rende il core!
I wait for death without alarm;	Ora il mio fine impavida,
Joy has replaced my sighing.	Piena di gioia attendo . . .
I'll say as I am dying	Potrò dirgli morendo:
That I have set him free!)	Salvo tu sei per me!)

COUNT

What does this mean? Come here to me,	Fra te che parli? . . . volgimi,
Repeat your solemn promise.	Volgimi il detto ancora,
Tell me I've not been dreaming,	O mi parrà delirio
Dreaming of folly and madness!	Quanto ascoltai finora . . .
You're mine, you're mine; repeat	[35] Tu mia! . . . tu mia! . . . ripetilo.
these words,	

That all my doubts may vanish.
I cannot yet believe
What you have said to me.

Il dubbio cor serena . . .
Ah! . . . ch'io lo credo appena
Udendolo da te!

LEONORA

Let's go! . . .

Andiam . . .

COUNT

Remember, you have sworn!

Giurasti . . . pensaci!

LEONORA

And I will keep my word.

È sacra la mia fe'!

(*They enter the tower.*)

Scene Three. *A gloomy dungeon. A barred window in one corner, a door at the back. A dimly burning lamp hangs from the ceiling. Azucena is lying on a kind of rough pallet. Manrico is seated beside her.* / *No. 14. Finale — Duet*

MANRICO

Mother, not sleeping?

Madre? . . . non dormi?

AZUCENA

Slumber still evades me,
This hateful night has been passed in
watching . . . praying . . .

L'invocai più volte,
Ma fugge il sonno a queste luci . . . Prego . . .

MANRICO

You are chilled by the dampness
And the cold around us?

L'aura fredda è molesta
Alle tue membra forse?

AZUCENA

No, but in this
Tomb of the living I feel my breath is stifled,
And I long to escape and gain my freedom.

No; da questa
Tomba di vivi solo fuggir vorrei,
Perchè sento il respiro soffocarmi!

MANRICO
(*wringing his hands*)

Escape!

Fuggir!

AZUCENA
(*rising*)

Do not lose courage.
My cruel tormentors have not long to
torture me!

Non attristarti:
Far di me strazio non potranno i crudi!

MANRICO

And why not?

Ah! come?

AZUCENA

See here . . . see upon my forehead
The hand of death has marked me,
My life is nearly ended.

Vedi . . . le sue fosche impronte
M'ha già segnato in fronte
Il dito della morte!

MANRICO

Ah!

Ahi!

AZUCENA

They'll find nothing
But a rotting corpse . . . frozen, motionless,
Hideous and horrible!

Troveranno
Un cadavere muto, gelido! . . . anzi
Uno scheletro!

MANRICO

Mother!

Cessa!

AZUCENA

You hear them? They are coming . . .
They will take me away . . . there in the fire
They'll burn me! My son, protect your
mother!

Non odi? . . . gente appressa . . .
I carnefici son . . . vogliono al rogo
Trarmi! . . . Difendi la tua madre!

MANRICO

There's no-one,   Alcuno,
Do not be frightened, there's no-one, I   Ti rassicura, qui non volge . . .
assure you.

AZUCENA
(Paying no attention to Manrico, in terror)

They'll burn me!   Il rogo!
What cruel torture!   Parola orrenda!

MANRICO

O mother, dear mother!   Oh madre! . . . oh madre!

AZUCENA

One morning   Un giorno,
Bloodthirsty murderers dragged my   Turba feroce l'ava tua condusse
mother from prison
To burn her! Look at all those flames   Al rogo! Mira la terribil vampa!
around her!
She is already on fire! Her hair is burning, [10] Ella n'è tocca già! già l'arso crine
The sparks fly up above her . . .   Al ciel manda faville! . . .
Her eyes are red with terror,   Osserva le pupille
And they start from their sockets! Ah! from Fuor dell'orbita lor! . . . ahi . . . chi mi toglie
this nightmare
Can no-one release me?   A spettacol sì atroce?

(She collapses in Manrico's arms in great distress.)

MANRICO

If your own son can still bring you   Se m'ami ancor, se voce
Comfort, if you are still the mother who Di figlio ha possa d'una madre in seno,
loved me,
Then forget all these horrors,   Ai terrori dell'alma
Come rest awhile and in slumber find peace Oblio cerca nel sonno, e posa e calma.
and solace.

(He leads her to the pallet.)

AZUCENA

Yes, let me sleep for my limbs are weary . . . [36] Sì, la stanchezza m'opprime, o figlio . . .
Then all these fears will no more come   Alla quiete io chiudo il ciglio . . .
near me . . .
But if that red fire once more be lighted, Ma se del rogo arder si veda
And you should see it, rouse me, I pray.   L'orrida fiamma, destami allor.

MANRICO

Come, close your eyes, and then in slumber [37] Riposa, o madre: Iddio conceda
Visions and fears will vanish away.   Men tristi immagini al tuo cor.

AZUCENA
(half sleeping, half waking)

Safe in our mountains, deep in Biscaya, [38] Ai nostri monti . . . ritorneremo . . .
New peace and solace we shall discover . . . L'antica pace . . . ivi godremo! . . .
There you will sing me songs of your   Tu canterai . . . sul tuo liuto . . .
childhood,
There I shall sleep again, far from all care. In sonno placido . . . io dormirò!

MANRICO

Rest now, dear mother, calm all your   Riposa, o madre: io prono e muto
terrors,
I know that Heaven will answer your prayer. La mente al cielo rivolgerò.

(Azucena falls asleep. Manrico remains on his knees beside her.)

Last Scene. *The door opens, and Leonora enters. The above, then the Count with an escort of Soldiers. / Recitative and Trio*

MANRICO

Ah! A light is glimmering on the stairway.   Che! . . . non m'inganno quel fioco lume?

LEONORA

At last, Manrico! Dear Manrico!   Son io, Manrico, mio Manrico!

MANRICO

My Leonora!   Oh, mia Leonora!
Ah! can it be that kind Heaven in mercy   Oh . . . mi concedi, pietoso Nume,
Sends me this blessing here before I die?   Gioia si grande, anzi ch'io mora?

LEONORA

You will not die . . . I've come to save you.   Tu non morrai . . . vengo a salvarti . . .

MANRICO

Save me? Leonora, how can you?   Come! . . . a salvarmi? . . . fia vero!

LEONORA

No questions,   Addio . . .
Don't lose a moment, goodbye now . . .   Tronca ogni indugio . . . t'affretta . . . parti!
hurry!

(She points to the door.)

MANRICO

You'll not come with me?   E tu non vieni?

LEONORA

No, I must stay here!   Restar degg'io!

MANRICO

But why?   Restar!

LEONORA

Go! Leave me!   Deh! fuggi! . . .

MANRICO

No.   No.

LEONORA
(trying to drag him through the door)

Go, I tell you!   Guai se tardi!

MANRICO

No!   No . . .

LEONORA

Save your life!   La tua vita!

MANRICO

My life is worthless.   [39]   Io la disprezzo!

LEONORA

Leave me, leave me! Go, I beg you!   Parti, parti, la tua vita!

MANRICO

But look this way and let me see you . . .   Pur figgi, o donna, in me gli sguardi! . . .
Who grants my freedom? What has it cost   Da chi l'avesti? ed a qual prezzo?
you?
You will not say? I need no answer . . .   Parlar non vuoi? Balen tremendo! . . .
It was my rival! I see it. I see it.   Dal mio rivale! Intendo intendo!
So you have sold yourself to that tyrant. [39]   Ha quest'infame l'amor venduto . . .
Sold him the love that you promised was   Venduto un core che mio giurò!
  mine.

74

Your anger blinds you and makes you heartless,

Yet far more cruel is your harsh injustice.

Stay here no longer; not even Heaven

Can now defend you! Go while there's time!

[40] Oh, come l'ira ti rende cieco!

Oh, quanto ingiusto, crudel sei meco!

T'arrendi, fuggi, o sei perduto!

Nemmeno il cielo salvar ti può!

(*Leonora throws herself at Manrico's feet.*)

AZUCENA
(*in her sleep*)

Safe in our mountains, deep in Biscaya,

New peace and happiness we shall discover . . .

There you will sing me songs of your childhood,

There I shall sleep again, far from all care.

[38] Ai nostri monti . . . ritorneremo . . .

L'antica pace . . . ivi godremo! . . .

Tu canterai . . . sul tuo liùto . . .

In sonno placido . . . io dormirò . . .

MANRICO

Now leave me!

Ti scosta!

LEONORA

Oh, be merciful . . .

See how I'm suffering . . . my strength Is failing.

Non respingermi . . .

Vedi? . . . languente, oppressa,
Io manco . . .

MANRICO

Go, I curse the day I ever met you.

Va' . . . ti abbomino . . .
Ti maledico . . .

LEONORA

Manrico,

Listen! Take back your curse, for you should pray

For me, to ask that Heaven

Grant me pardon!

Ah, cessa!

Non d'imprecar, di volgere

Per me la prece a Dio

È questa l'ora!

MANRICO

That Heaven grant you Pardon? What's this you tell me?

Un brivido

Corse nel petto mio!

LEONORA
(*She falls on her face.*)

Manrico!

Manrico!

MANRICO

Dear one, speak to me . . .

Tell me.

Donna! svelami . . .

Narra.

LEONORA

Death has come to take me!

Ho la morte in seno.

MANRICO

You're dying!

La morte! . . .

LEONORA

Yes! For this poison here

Has reached my heart more swiftly Than I imagined!

Ah! fu più rapida

La forza del veleno
Ch'io non pensava!

MANRICO

Can this be true?

Oh fulmine!

LEONORA

Touch me, my hands are frozen . . .

Senti! la mano è gelo . . .
(*touching her breast*)

| But here, within me, a fire is
Burning! | Ma qui ... qui foco terribil
Arde! |

MANRICO

| Why have you done this? | Che festi! ... o cielo! |

LEONORA

| Rather than live to be his bride,
I die for you my love ... | [41] Prima che d'altri vivere ...
Io volli tua morir! |

MANRICO

| What madness that I have dared to curse
This angel from above. | Insano! ... ed io quest'angelo
Osava maledir! |

LEONORA

| My sight is failing ... | Più non resisto! |

MANRICO

| I doubted you! | Ahi misera! ... |

(*The Count enters, and stops on the threshold.*)

LEONORA

| My life is over ... I'm dying ... | Ecco l'istante! ... io moro ... |

(*holding out her right hand to him in farewell*)

| Manrico! O Heavenly Father,
Pardon this humble sinner ...
Rather ... than ... live to be his bride ...
I die ... for you my love! | Manrico! Or la tua grazia ...
Padre del cielo ... imploro ...
Prima ... che ... d'altri vivere ...
Io volli ... tua morir! |

(*She dies.*)

COUNT

| (This woman has deluded me,
And dies to save his life!) | (Ah! volle me deludere,
E per costui morir!) |

(*pointing out Manrico to the Soldiers*)

| Behead the traitor! | Sia tratto al ceppo! |

MANRICO
(*as he is led out by the Soldiers*)

| Mother, farewell for ever! | Madre! ah madre, addio! |

AZUCENA
(*waking*)

| Manrico! My son, where are you? | Manrico! Ov'è mio figlio? |

COUNT

| They execute him. | A morte corre! ... |

AZUCENA

| Have mercy! ... listen ... | Ah ferma! ... M'odi! |

COUNT
(*dragging Azucena to the window*)

| Look there! | Vedi! |

AZUCENA

| Stop them! | Cielo! |

COUNT

| He's perished! | È spento! |

AZUCENA

| Manrico was your brother! | Egli era tuo fratello! ... |

COUNT

| Ah! Barbarous fate! | Ei! ... quale orror! |

AZUCENA

You are avenged, o mother!   Sei vendicata, o madre!

(*She collapses beneath the window.*)

COUNT
(*aghast*)

And I live on!   E vivo ancor!

Curtain.

Fiorenza Cossotto as Azucena at Covent Garden in 1965 (photo: Donald Southern)

Discography *by Martin Hoyle* The specialist is referred to *Opera on Record* (ed. Alan Blyth, Hutchinson 1979) for detailed analysis. The following list is a selective discography of available complete recordings, in stereo and sung in Italian.

Conductor Company/Orchestra	*Karajan* La Scala, Milan	*Erede* Geneva, Grand Theatre	*Bonynge* London Opera Chorus National PO	*Mehta* Ambrosian Opera Chorus New Phil.	*Karajan* Deutsche Oper Chorus Berlin PO
Manrico	Di Stefano	Del Monaco	Pavarotti	Domingo	Bonisolli
Leonora	Callas	Tebaldi	Sutherland	L. Price	L. Price
Luna	Panerai	Savarese	Wixell	Milnes	Cappucilli
Azucena	Barbieri	Simionato	Horne	Cossotto	Obraztsova
Disc UK Number	SLS869	GOS614-6	D82D3	SER5586-8	SLS5111
Tape UK Number	TC-SLS869		K82K32	RK40002	TC-SLS5111
Excerpts disc		SPA513	SET631		
Excerpts tape		KCSP513	KCET631		
Disc US number			Lon-13124	LSC6194	SX-3855
Tape US number			513124		4X3X-3855
Excerpts disc (US)				LSC3203	
Excerpts tape (US)				RK-1197	

Conductor Company/Orchestra	*Davis* **Royal Opera, Covent Garden**	*Basile* **Rome Opera**	*Serafin* **La Scala, Milan**
Manrico	Carrerras	Tucker	Bergonzi
Leonora	Ricciarelli	L. Price	Stella
Luna	Mazurok	Warren	Bastianini
Azucena	Toczska	Elias	Cossotto
Disc UK number	6769 063		
Tape UK number	7654 063		
Excerpts disc			
Excerpts tape			
Disc US number	6769 063	AGL3-4146	2728008
Tape US Number	7654 063	AGL3-4146	3373008
Excerpts disc (US)			
Excerpts tape (US)			

Bibliography

The opera is studied by Julian Budden in the second volume of his three-volume classic work on *The Operas of Verdi* (Cassell, 1978). It is obviously mentioned in all the other biographies of the composer (for instance, Francis Toye 1931, Frank Walker 1962) and the important letters which Verdi wrote at the time of the composition are contained in Charles Osborne's translation of them (Gollancz, 1971). Other contemporary sources and beautiful illustrations may be found in William Weaver's *Verdi: A Documentary Study* (Thames & Hudson, 1977). Gabriele Baldini's *The Story of Giuseppe Verdi* is available in an English translation by Roger Parker (Cambridge, 1980).

There is no biography of Cammarano, or García Gutiérrez.

Contributors

Marcello Conati, after a career as repetiteur and vocal coach, became archivist to the Institute for Verdi Studies in Parma (1971-1978) and is currently working on an edition of Verdi's letters.

D.R.B. Kimbell, Professor of Music at the University of St Andrews, is the author of *Verdi and the Age of Romanticism*.

Donald Shaw is Professor of Hispanic Studies at the University of Edinburgh.

Sherrill Milnes and Irina Archipova at Covent Garden in 1975 (photo: Anthony Crickmay)